Pacific Northwest Foraging Field Guide

A Beginner's Foraging Guidebook for Finding,
Identifying, Harvesting, and Preparing Wild Edible
Plants of North America

By

Kennard Wheatly

Disclaimer

This book offers knowledgeable and trustworthy information on the subject area discussed. Nevertheless, the opinions presented in this work belong solely to the author and are not intended to be considered expert advice or counsel. The reader is therefore accountable for his/ her own decision.

Table of Contents

Introduction

The Pacific Northwest region of North America is known for its diverse and abundant flora, making it a prime location for foraging enthusiasts. Whether you're a seasoned forager or a beginner looking to explore the bounty of wild edible plants, the "Pacific Northwest Foraging Field Guide" is an essential companion.

This guidebook is designed to help you identify, harvest, and prepare wild edible plants found throughout the Pacific Northwest region, including parts of Alaska, Washington, Oregon, Idaho, Montana, and British Columbia. It covers several species of plants, including fruits, nuts, berries, mushrooms, greens, and roots, with detailed descriptions and photographs to aid identification.

The historical and cultural significance of wild edible plants in the Pacific Northwest is worth considering, as well as how to sustainably harvest and care for the plants you gather. Also, the plant descriptions in the guidebook are organized by season, allowing you to easily find what's available at any given time. Each entry includes a detailed description of the plant, including its habitat, identifying features, and traditional uses. Also included are tips on when and how to harvest each plant and how to prepare it for consumption.

With this guide, you will realize that foraging is beyond just a recreational activity. It is an excellent way to connect with nature and appreciate what she provides. The importance of foraging with care and respect for the environment should not be undervalued because we are guests in the plants' natural habitats.

Another standout feature of the "Pacific Northwest Foraging Field Guide" is its emphasis on safety. There are clear guidelines for identifying poisonous plants and avoiding potentially harmful species. Also, carefully outlined steps have been curated for preparing the most flavorful recipes from these wild plants for food and medicine.

Chapter 1

Fundamentals of Foraging Wild Plants

What is Foraging?

Before the advent of civilization, our ancestors dedicated a vital part of their existence to getting an essential physiological need, food, through unique ways. Regardless of the dangers in their surrounding, they took their time to hunt animals on land and water skillfully and patiently.

They had access to fresh meat from antelopes, rabbits, and even lions making them involved in the preparation process from start to finish. These humans would venture deep into forests, wilderness, or thick bushes to gather herbs, fruits, and seeds for survival. Little wonder they enjoyed good health, longevity, strength, and remarkable intelligence.

The rise of civilization and increasing technological advancements in our modern world have brought about new dynamics in how we get food. In highly developed countries like the United States, people get food readily from fast food restaurants, grocery stores, or through a simple click on the phone from a food delivery service.

We have very little knowledge about the food we consume, and this knowledge is limited to what we see on attractive wrappers or packages. Their usual pattern involves shopping for food, preparing it, eating it, and waiting for it to digest. Only very few people have developed a personal connection with their food.

Breaking free from this neverending cycle of ignorance is now made possible by a blooming environment movement that educates society on venturing into growing their food. One excellent benefit of adopting this culture is that local agriculture will be more recognized and given all the support it deserves. Furthermore, the concept of foraging, which involves searching for wild food, is gaining more popularity among individuals who strive to eat in a way that promotes the conservation of our natural environment.

At first, you may think that foraging is only possible in places known to be wild, like thick bushes or forests.

However, it would interest you to know that foraging is possible even in urban areas, including our cities. You can actively forage for food in the cities by maximizing the green spaces near you. These green spaces include your front or backyards and the parks near you. You can find mushrooms, fresh berries, and other healthy greens in rural and urban areas. However, these plants are more abundant in rural settings.

People have different reasons for venturing into the culture of foraging. You might forage food for leisure and recreation. Foraging can also be a means to explore your natural environment and gain more knowledge about naturally occurring foods. People are also motivated to forage for food due to the numerous health benefits of eating these naturally occurring foods.

What Are Wild Edible Plants?
A careful study into the remarkable ability of humans to quickly adapt to their natural environment for survival throughout history points to the dependence on wild plants and animals. Early humans were excellent at observing their environment and predicting the best

time to plant, harvest, set traps, hunt the forest, and even go fishing.

As man evolved to become a more complex entity, many wild plant species have assumed an essential role in aiding human survival by serving as food and medicines. There are unique plants all over the world that are known to have the ability to cure many types of illnesses or diseases. Our ancestors had physicians or well-known herbalists who founded apothecaries and were very knowledgeable about several medicinal and toxic herbs. This is known as alternative medicine today.

If you wish to gain an understanding of wild edible plants, start by picturing shrubs, farmlands, uncultivated land areas, bushes, or anything that defines the natural environment with greens. Any plant species that occupy these habitats and adapt in their peculiar way are known as wild plants. These plants can be recognized as wild edible plants if they can be ingested as a whole or in parts without causing harm.

In addition, the different parts of these plants, such as the stems, roots, leaves, seeds, and even flowers, are packed with numerous nutrients, minerals, and vitamins necessary for the normal functioning of the human body. The nutritional benefits make it perfect for decreasing the risk of developing malnutrition, illnesses, or terminal disease such as cancer in the future.

Also, these wild edible plants have features that make them stand out from other popular plants. These features include the possession of either one or all of the following:

- Leaflets that share a common stalk. This is also called a compound leaf.
- Well-structured massive roots.
- Grown seeds.
- Ariel shoots.
- Variation in fragrance and color.

We cannot ignore the numerous benefits of wild edible plants. Most rural areas feed heavily on staple foods, majorly rice, corn, and wheat. So they rely on these plants to have a nutritionally adequate diet and combat hunger during emergencies and famine. Wild edible plants are readily available, free of cost during any season, and provide immense support for communities with a high population of poor and marginalized families. More importantly, families in urbanized areas can supplement the high amounts of processed foods that have become the mainstay of societies with fresh wild edible plants.

Why Forage Wild Plants?

We have so far set the ball in motion by understanding the importance of wild edible plants for food and medicine. However, people often wonder why forage wild plants, especially in developed countries, when food and drugs can be purchased easily from a store or a modern pharmacy with a prescription.

Think about our ancestors who were skilled hunter-gatherers. These humans rarely had to deal with the diseases that have become an issue of concern worldwide today. Well-known life-threatening diet-related illnesses include obesity, diabetes, cancer, and heart-related diseases. One way to learn the knowledge they had concerning eating healthy is by foraging. By so doing, we can re-establish a deeper connection with what goes into our bodies.

Despite the outstanding medicinal properties of most wild plants, foraging them should not be a means to replace conventional. Instead, it helps us make these plants part of our daily diet. Here are carefully outlined reasons why you should forage wild plants.

1. Highest-Quality Botanicals

Foraging for wild plants exposes us to a wide range of beneficial plant species. Plants cultivated in farms are not bad themselves, just that they cannot match up to the potency of these foraged plants. A good example is when you try extracting oil from dried St. John's Worth or Violet leaves which play an essential role in alternative medicine. After extraction, you would most likely process oil with an unsatisfactory red color. This is because the dried St. John's Worth and Red Violet have fewer active components compared to the dense nutritional value of the fresh plant.

2. Nature's Abundance

This is one beautiful reason to forage wild plants. Nature has given us these edible plants in abundance and free of charge. Even when we run out of cash, we do not need to break the bank to return home with a basket full of wild edible and medicinal plants like Chickweed or Nettle greens. You can bypass local foods from grocery stores or farms and venture into the abundance nature offers at no cost.

3. Wild Food Security

Beyond feeding numerous families on a pocket-friendly budget, wild edible plants are an excellent means to sustain communities by providing food security during periods of famine. "The wild weed crops create a net of security for local communities when other sources of food are minimal or scarce" (Katrina Blair, 2014). Undoubtedly, foraging can be stressful and time-consuming, but it is worth the try. You get far greater value in both quality and quantity than what you would get in a big bag of dried herbs bought from a grocery store.

4. Connection With Local Plants

Another good reason to forage wild plants is to establish a personal connection with them. Enhancing focus on naturally occurring plants in our immediate environment is known as "bioregional herbalism." Constantly exploring the vast species of wild plants helps us to learn from them and maximize their benefits. Also, we will appreciate their existence and work towards promoting the ecological relationships between humans and nature. This will undoubtedly give us a sense of responsibility for our modern world.

5. Sustainability

You can promote a sustainable environment by committing yourself to foraging wild edible plants. With foraging, there will be a significant reduction in the use of plastic bags for packaging and the use of fossil fuels for transportation which contributes to the pollution of the environment. Also, you will get your foods fresh, healthy, and in their raw botanical form, promoting Zero-Waste Herbalism.

6. Connecting With Nature

You can take foraging to the next level by using it as a channel to get the best out of nature. An outstanding practice developed in Japan during the 1980s called Forest Bathing, known as Shinrin-yoku by locals, involves deliberately exploring your natural environment. Opening your mind, body, and soul to nature promotes relaxation and reduces stress. This practice got the attention of researchers who discovered a connection between forest bathing and its impact on the human system.

The numerous benefits include promoting immunity, improving heart function, and preventing respiratory diseases. It improves concentration and mood and promotes relaxation. Also, it promotes positive thinking and gives one a sense of fulfillment by reducing stress levels.

According to the authors, the total population of humans throughout history in conjunction with nature is less than 0.01%, which leaves the remaining species making up nature at 99.99%. This great difference draws humans to where they began their primal nature.

People who have established a connection with nature by embracing the practice of foraging have never looked back. The whole process, from start to finish, is rewarding and gives a deep sense of self-actualization. We can draw strength and value our existence by connecting with nature.

7. Expanding Your Palate

You can go beyond your usual everyday foods to feed your palate something new and exciting by eating wild edible plants alongside your dishes. The typical lifestyle of populations occupying industrialized areas of the world involves rushing to work and trying so hard to meet up with deadlines. It is a struggle with time. This prompts most people to go the easy and fast way of consuming highly processed foods with increasing health risks and placing less value on nutrition.

Also, most people eat sweet and salty foods over foods with bitter flavors. It would interest you to know that bitter plants are excellent for promoting digestive and liver function. As Herbalists Guido Masé (2013) rightly explains, the pursuit of making food easier to prepare and consume through centralization and industrialization of food processing has caused more harm than good. Introducing intense flavors and bitter herbs to our diet will help us revisit the kind of meal our ancestors once lived on. By so doing, we can enjoy all the nutrients, vitamins, and minerals available during their unique era, helping us live healthily.

Chapter 2

Getting Ready to Forage

When to Forage

Foraging is an exciting activity unhindered by time or season and is considered by many to provide excellent food security during food scarcity or famine. Foraging during winter will not leave your basket empty or overflowing with wild edibles. However, the total quantity of foraged food will be much lower. In addition, you may spend long hours trying to get the same proportion of yield you would get during spring or summer.

The most favorable time to forage for wild foods in terms of quality and quantity is during spring and early autumn/late summer. Spring, for instance, is the best time to forage for rich leafy greens and edible herbaceous plants with dense nutrients. While during Summer, you can get a wide variety of freshly ripened berries and fruits. Also, the best fungi species are seen easily during autumn. During these periods, you can get a broad range of plant species blooming and packed with the best nutrients in their peak values.

Another factor that favors excellent foraging results is location. A good example is that the South experience spring earlier than areas in the North, giving the South an edge for quality foraging before the North could experience such. Also, the natural environment and the habitat where you can find your preferred wild edibles determine how well you can forage.

Finding Where to Forage

Foraging can be done in several locations or natural environments that propel wild edibles to thrive. These environments include:

1. Your garden, either in your front or backyard. You can cultivate any specie of wild edibles to have long-lasting access to fresh and healthy foods.

2. Verges or hedgerows close to your home. This is another good place to find wild food. It houses so many wild plant species. And in some locations,

you might find a particular type of species dominating others.

3. Some public parks or common lands are also home to wild plants which can be actively foraged. These places are packed with many green areas and are occupied by a dense population of wild edibles.

4. Public paths through agricultural land or farmlands.

5. Forests or woodlands, where you can find limitless varieties of wild foods that can be foraged without any hindrance.

6. Coastlines, where you can forage edibles that need a constant water supply to grow and populate quickly.

Before going out to forage on any private land, you should always seek a go-ahead or permission from the land owner before foraging for edibles. This will ensure you do not end up on the wrong side of the law and get sanctioned for trespassing. If you are uncertain about the local status and several laws that guide the concept of foraging in a particular location or area of land, do not hesitate to ask questions before venturing into your newfound hobby.

Numerous nature reserves permit foraging for personal recreational purposes (responsible foraging) and not for commercial purposes. This principle is also applicable to National Trust Properties, but you should never forget to fact-check the regulations that guide foraging in your preferred site.

Sustainable and Ethical Foraging Practices

1. Get Permission

Even though foraging is maximizing what nature has given us free of charge without limitations, it is necessary to get prior permission before going to forage on private land.

Always let the owner know that your sole purpose on that land is to forage for wild edibles while maintaining total respect for the land. You should take only what you have described to the landowner to earn their trust.

In addition, you can offer little gifts like jelly, jam, tea, or something worthwhile in return for the access granted to forage.

The local statutes, rules, or regulations guiding the use of public lands, such as state and national forest reserves, national parks, etc., vary across different locations. You might require a permit to forage in some of these locations, but in others, you can freely use the land. Some places limit the number of wild edibles you can forage in pounds or kilograms.

In some parks, certain wild plant species gets more priority over another; for example, some parks instruct foragers to harvest berries but leave out mushrooms. Do not leave the land area without double-checking to ensure you follow the rules thoroughly.

2. Correctly Identify Wild Edible Plants

Before you begin harvesting any wild plant at your desired location, ensure that such plant is not only edible but also safe. Make sure you correctly identify any plant before harvesting. Doing this will ensure you avoid picking poisonous or toxic plants disguised as wild edibles.

When you wish to go foraging for some mushrooms, it is advisable to harvest a single specie for immediate use and return later to pick out more. This is to promote the sustainability of the natural habitat of those plant species. Leaving certain plants untouched will encourage them to grow, reproduce and thrive.

3. Never Harvest the Only Plant

Try as much as possible to also look out for nature while foraging. If you find only a single plant species in an area of land, try to size up the total population to determine how well you harvest such edible. For species with low populations, it is advisable to let them be to allow time to grow and increase in population.

For species with a sizable population, ensure you do not harvest all the plants; it would not be nice to have medicinal edibles go extinct. Remember that the animals, forests, and even the earth as a planet depends on these plant species to survive as much as we do.

Another essential practice is to forage from different spots. Never pick out all edibles in a single spot. For example, if you find ten wild edibles along the same line, seek to pick out only 10% of the total population of plant specie. This should be nothing less than one edible in a spot per line.

4. Harvest Edible Plants Wisely

It is necessary to forage wisely to benefit greatly. Ensure to scrutinize the wild edible plants you come across before harvesting them. Avoid picking out unhealthy-looking plants due to flooding, drought, fire, or any similar disaster. As was earlier mentioned, select plant species that are abundant and of excellent quality. Harvesting inferior plants would diminish the nutrients you would have gotten from a healthy plant.

When your foraging activity is channeled at only harvesting plant parts, ensure to harvest the top two-thirds (2/3) of the whole plant, leaving the remaining to grow and multiply. Anytime you need just the root, there is no need to be confused. Simply dig up the plant carefully and precisely, then cut portions of this root with a sharp knife, leaving the rest to mother earth.

Being fully responsible and carefully abiding by foraging principles contributes to the health of plants during the next harvest. Remember the practice discussed earlier called Forest Bathing? Take time to apply this concept to your foraging adventures while making the experience exciting, safe, and enabling for the earth.

5. Take Only the Amount Needed

Once again, when foraging, consider other factors like environmental and plant sustainability. This will ensure you do not pick out more than the required amount. If you plan to make a berry jam from foraged berries, endeavor to pick out the precise quantity needed to make specific jars of berry jam.

You do not need to store more than the required quantity at home because mother earth requires these plants also for sustenance. You can always return to find them refreshed, renewed, and in excellent quality.

Safe Practices When Foraging

You must be familiar with certain safety measures before you embark on a foraging activity. We will carefully outline these safety measures below.

Firstly, there are some different species of wild plants. Some are easily identifiable, while others are difficult to identify. Also, some plants are undoubtedly packed with many health benefits, while some are toxic to the human body if ingested by accident; therefore, you must never eat any wild plant that you cannot 100% positively identify. Remember, being careless about this might result in severe consequences.

In addition, to ensure safety, especially as a newbie in the foraging field, you can embark on this expedition with an expert or professional forager. Another option is to consult or read a lot of verifiable resources or books to help you identify these plants effortlessly. Thankfully this book has a comprehensible collection of popular wild food that is easily identifiable and safe for consumption. On the other hand, the universal edibility test can come in handy when you are in a dire situation while foraging in the wild and you don't have any guide with you to assist

Secondly, human activities can pollute wild edibles, especially in highly populated areas. It is advisable to forage in areas with a relatively low human population, areas with very little proximity to industries, busy streets, or other sources capable of causing pollution. Doing so will ensure you find the best range of wild edibles. Also, take into consideration the areas of land that are prone to contamination from industrial chemicals or deposits. Aerosols like pesticides and herbicides on wild edibles are also harmful to health.

Also, you need to apply simple logic when foraging wild edibles. Something as simple as wearing long-sleeved clothing, gloves, long skirts or trousers, and some protective boots can protect you from thorny plants, stinging plants such as nettles, and plants that cause hypersensitivity reactions. A typical example is the Gaint Hogweed which foragers should be wary of due to its phototoxic sap, capable of causing painful blisters and scars.

Another safe practice when foraging in a wild environment is to take account of the weather conditions and tide before heading out.

Chapter 3

Foraging in Spring

Stinging Nettles

Identifying Stinging Nettles

Identifying a stinging nettle is not so difficult due to its unique appearance. Its leaves are pubescent (hairy) and bright green, and sometimes there might be a hint of purple color. This plant grows on snow or fertile soil in late January, especially in the Pacific Northwest. The stinging quality of Nettle is from the strongly serrated edges, which become more conspicuous as this plant develops.

The nettle leaf is heart-shaped with a characteristic small stem that links the top of the heart-shaped leaf to the central stem. The spiky base of the leaf faces away from the main stem. The leaves are arranged in pairs on this plant's central stem, each in opposite directions, and positioned at 12 and 6 o'clock. The next set beneath is slightly larger at 3 and 9 o'clock positions. The next set below is much larger than the previous set, positioning at 12 and 6 o'clock. The pattern keeps going till it reaches a terminal point close to its roots.

The nettles reach about 3 to 6 feet high or more during late spring. The largest of its leaves take their place on the top of the plant, with a length of 7 inches. And you will find flowers in beautiful greenish/whitish clusters, which will become seeds and change their color to a slightly brownish hue.

As autumn draws nearer, the leaves will wither and fall due to insufficient light and water for photosynthesis.

After, the color of the stems will change from bright green to brown, then to whitish grey as winter finally shows its face. The bare stalks are not left out as they may decompose before the underground rhizomes sprout new leaves. These stalks may also remain intact to pioneer the emergence of a new generation of foliage.

In case you still doubt the identity of the stinging nettle, go ahead to touch it and see the result for yourself. You should feel a sting almost immediately, and when you observe the area on your skin, you should see a small red welt. If nothing like that happens after touching the plant, you could consult a field guide for additional information to help you confirm the plant's identity. A popular guide is the Plants of the Pacific Northwest Coast, written by Pojar and MacKinnon.

When to Harvest Stinging Nettle?

Young nettles emerging

Nettles can be harvested when new leaves begin to sprout from the ground. This can continue until the flowers have gone to seed during the late fall; however, foragers must harvest before the stems start to rot due to rainfall. You can forage at your own pace and convenience.

This wild edible is ideal for making many delicacies and healthy tea, so pick the nettle leaves before they start flowering. There are speculations concerning ingesting a flowered nettle, and one such is that bladder stones or cystoliths, which are harmful to the urinary tract, might form. Many resources on the internet agree with this speculation. However, it is not scientifically verifiable, making the information more of an assumption than a fact.

However, since so many believe that flowering nettles are terrible for the kidneys, it is advisable to stick to harvesting the leaves before they begin flowering. Till proper scientific research is made to verify or disregard this assumption, it is better to be cautious.

Nettles beginning to bloom: Do not harvest for food or medicine during/ after this stage, except in emergencies

Hardly or never would you find nettles maturing or developing in the same place. Each plant attains its unique reproductive stage based on location, overstory, substrate, etc. After carefully observing the land filled with nettles, you will discover that some are ready to be harvested, while others need more time. Nettles that have begun seeding are not useless, and you can pick the stems for rope-making before the rain spurs them to decay.

How to Harvest Stinging Nettle?

The answer is pretty straightforward. Before heading out, wear long sleeves, long pants or skirts, and protective gloves. While harvesting the leaves, make use of scissors and not your hands. Understanding how the stinging process works will make your experience of foraging nettles more interesting.

During a close-up inspection of stinging nettle, you will notice tiny hairs on the leaves and stems. Never make the mistake of underestimating these hairs that seem harmless because they can penetrate the skin, break off and trigger the formation of formic acid, which gives off a stinging sensation.

It is unknown if every hair on the nettle leaf is hollow or if any hair contains formic acid. One thing is that the lightest touch can sting, but sometimes, you need more than a slight touch to experience a sting. The arrangement of the hairs is a pointer to getting stung or not. Take a nettle leaf and observe the direction the hairs are facing. You will notice that they point from the top to the bottom of the point of the leaf. The trick to avoiding getting stung is to run your hands from the cleft portion to the bottom; otherwise, you will end up with hairs stuck in your skin.

Now let us be more practical; if you wish to harvest some nettle leaves but have no scissors at hand, you can apply a simple trick dependent on the fact that the nettle hairs point downwards from top to bottom. After noting how much you wish to pick out, place your thumb and index fingers above and below the leaf. With those fingers, give the leaf a slight pinch by pressing the hairs flat to prevent any possibility of getting poked.

Harvesting the leaves one at a time can be time-consuming, but you must endeavor to apply caution. After selecting your leaf as described above and giving it a gentle pinch, take note of the location and orientation of nearby leaves. Smaller leaves above the one you intend to harvest can prick the top of your hand when you attempt to pull it out of the stem. Be mindful of the larger bottom leaves that target your wrist as you focus on the cunning upper leaves. The sting of a nettle plant is swift and painful.

What Part of Stinging Nettle Do I Harvest?

Harvesting the top leaves that are said to be tender is recommended. That is, about two to three pairs of the leaf are ideal for making food. Before harvesting the leaves, you should watch for nettles that might have been a snack for butterfly larvae and moths. These species feed on nettles and leave visible holes, blackened areas, and waste materials on the leaves. Harvest the first leaf set on the terminal bud if you come across young nettles. Doing so will trigger the lateral bud to grow, giving the plant room to become bushier and providing you with a continuous harvest.

Harvest the entire stem of the nettle plant if you need fiber. To do this, clip the stem near the ground, and with gloved hands, grasp the bottom and run your gloved hand from the bottom to the top so you can detach the leaves seamlessly. Strip off the leaves at the site where you decide to forage to allow the remaining leaves to decompose and nourish the soil for the next generation of nettles.

Processing Stinging Nettles for Food

Finally, you have harvested some nettles. Now it's time to move on to the next part, "how to process these leaves into nutritious food." If you use them immediately, spread the leaves on a clean surface for a while to give time for tiny critters or insects to escape. After giving these creatures a chance at freedom, run the leaves beneath cold tap water. This will wash away any debris, leaving the leaves clean and ready for processing.

If you wish to use the leaves as they are, regardless of an extra protein or a little dirt, feel free to do so. However, avoid putting the leaves directly into a salad as an ingredient so your guest will not regret visiting you for dinner. Even though you can do without gloves at this stage, you should use them while handling these leaves. You can preserve freshly harvested and unwashed nettles in your refrigerator for about two to three days. With proper storage, you can access fresh leaves at any time.

Dry nettles are great for making tea. To dry the moist leaves, put them in a clean paper bag, place the bag in front of a furnace and allow the warm air to soak up the moisture. Remember, do not stir the leaves while moist to avoid getting stung. Dry leaves lose their ability to sting because the hairs shrivel up, making them safe to handle. Ensure not to dry the leaves excessively because they begin to burn or lose their green color.

There are other safer methods to dry nettle leaves, like using a dehydrator or hanging them outside to let nature do the job. Once the leaves are properly dried, store them in a glass jar and take scoops to make your tea. Some people prefer making tea from fresh nettle leaves, which is fine. You can explore the dry or raw leaves to suit your taste.

You can freeze your foraged nettles to use them all year round. Start by putting the fresh leaves in a food processor and blending until they are finely chopped. Put the shredded leaves in clean containers and store them in the freezer until when needed. Handling chopped nettles with bare hands is safe because the food processor has been able to break the hairs, thereby making it lose the ability to sting.

Some people blanch the nettles before using them by pouring them into boiling water and then tossing them into cold water. The blanching method comes with a disadvantage; several nutrients that cannot survive heat are destroyed in the process of blanching in hot water.

Dandelions

Dandelions (Taraxacum officinale) are undoubtedly beautiful, with brightly colored flowers and spiky leaves that are very popular and easy to identify. Every part of the dandelion, from the flowers, leaves, and stems to roots, are edible with numerous medical benefits. It is a perennial herb but classified as a weed with several medicinal and culinary uses. This widely spread plant is the best to forage for those new to the world of foraging.

Where and When to Find Dandelions

Dandelions can thrive on all seven continents worldwide and under any climate. During autumn and spring, dandelions reach the peak of their maturity. However, in warmer weather conditions, they develop well throughout the year. In addition, their leaves are very tender during spring, making it the ideal time to harvest them.

This plant is widely spread and distributed along gardens, lawns, meadows, parks, pastures, etc. Although dandelions may thrive better under shade due to the coolness it permits, they also grow well beneath direct sunlight.

Identifying Dandelion

Dandelions are easy to identify. With their yellow blooms and leaves, which you can find at the bottom of the stem, you can easily distinguish them from other plants. Its flowers grow on a single thin stem that does not branch, and it has lobed leaves which produce sap with a milky color.

The seed head, in particular, is popular among children. The memory of making a wish and going ahead to blow the white puffball as a child is soothing. The root is long and responsible for propelling nutrients to other parts of the plant. A good thing about the root is that it can be roasted and used as a substitute for caffeinated coffee.

Harvesting Dandelions

Harvesting dandelions is not a problem at all due to how widely spread they are. They can be found anywhere, from lawns to parks and so on. Because of how common this plant is, you should be wary of possible pesticide and herbicide use on the plants, especially in industrial areas.

It is better to forage for unsprayed dandelions on your lawn, a friend's, or a neighbor's property. Always endeavor to show appreciation after foraging on another person's property. You can do that by giving gifts created from your foraged plant, such as soap made from dandelion, and seeing their faces beam in appreciation.

The best time to pick dandelions is in the morning when the flowers are open and dry. Also, look out for big leaves with few lobes because they taste better than those with little lobes. Spread the plants on a drying screen or flat surface if you need dried dandelions. You should ensure close monitoring to avoid over-drying the plants and having only the puffballs left. Limit the total drying time to about one to two days. However, if you wish to use the fresh leaves instead, you can store them in the freezer until they are ready for consumption.

Chickweed

Where And When to Look for Chickweed

The common chickweed specie, Stellaria media, has become a natural plant species in North America. You will most likely find it in your lawn; usually, they grow on cool and moist soil.

An ideal time to forage for chickweed is when they bloom, which is early spring, and one way to identify them is by looking out for small white flowers. It thrives well in damp areas with shade and shelter, but there is a marked decrease in growth when the peak of summer hits.

Chickweed is believed to be a weed like other wild edibles because they grow among flowers and vegetables in the garden. Most gardeners find that disappointing. You can pull out as much chickweed as possible to give room for your vegetables so they can grow well without much competition. You can create your chickweed garden if you do not like going into the woods or picking them out from your vegetable garden.

Identifying Chickweed

This small annual plant is a well-known European native that thrives well on cool, moisture-rich soil. This medicinal weed is usually at its peak stage and repopulates during early spring and late fall. You can find a small chickweed population during summer and winter. They grow in your cold frames, garden beds, fences, and barns.

The Stem

The first thing to note when trying to identify chickweed is its stem. It stands out from other weeds by having a single line of short fine hairs running along each side of the stem. Anytime the row of fine hairs comes in contact with a leaf, the hairs migrate to the other side of the stem. However, chickweed stems are not covered in these hairs.

Sometimes, you might have difficulty trying to see it with your eyes alone. A good solution is to take a picture of the stem using your phone, then zoom the photo on the stem area; this will help you visualize it better to locate the fine hairs. As for the color of the stems, they usually exist in shades of burgundy or green.

Still, on the stem, no chickweed stem has sap oozing from it. The moment you break one and find out you can see traces of white sap, disregard the possibility of it being chickweed. It has an inedible look-alike called spurge (Euphorbia spp).

The Leaves

The shape of a chickweed leaf is usually oval or eggs shaped. These leaves tend to grow opposite each other on the stem. Another distinguishing feature is the presence of stalks; the upper leaves do not possess stalks, while the lower leaves have stalks. Chickweed leaves exist in green colors and are without hair. However, you might find some fine hairs on the base of the leaf, and the green parts (sepals) that cover the flowers are with fine hairs.

The Flowers

The flowers of this plant are small and have a satisfying white color. The petals are five in number, but because they are deeply divided, they look like they are ten in number. Stellaris is the Latin name of the chickweed flower, which means star; this describes the physical appearance of the small white flowers.

For those unsure about the identity of chickweed, it is advisable to patiently wait for the flowers to bloom, which is one of the key identifiers, before picking it up. The major look-alike of this plant is the scarlet pimpernel (Anagallis arvensis), which has reddish-orange flowers and is unhealthy to eat.

Harvesting Chickweed

Harvesting chickweed is very easy. With your hands, grab a handful of your desired quantity and snip it with scissors. If you do not have scissors, you can make do with your hands by pinching them off the stem. People usually prefer to eat the top one-fourth to one-third.

You might find chickweed often entwined with other plants in your garden. So remember that when foraging for chickweed, you would be harvesting it alongside that plant. The ideal period to harvest chickweed is when it is still tender and young. Aged chickweed that has probably gone to seed and become yellow is not edible.

Chickweed has a high water content and should be dried before infusing it into oils and salves.

Drying Chickweed

Pour and spread your freshly foraged chickweed on a dying screen, dish towel, or paper towel in a single layer. Ensure enough room or space on the drying screen for proper air circulation. Herbs that are laid in several layers usually begin to generate heat and become compost. Another alternative to drying using natural air is to use a dehydrator. Set the machine to a temperature of 95^0F for a few hours. After drying, you will notice that the herb has probably shrunk significantly, to your surprise. This is normal because chickweed has a lot of water content.

After drying thoroughly, you can store the herb in a glass jar or paper bag and keep it in a cool, dry area away from direct sunlight. The dried herb is not ideal for all-year-round usage because it could start to turn brown or give off a musty smell. As long as it maintains a green color with its natural scent, you can keep using it; otherwise, you should dispose of it as compost.

Lambs Quarter

Where to Find Wild Spinach

Lamb quarters, also known as wild spinach, often inhabit areas with moist and fertile soil. You will find them thriving well in farms and gardens with nitrogen-rich soil, which explains why locals call them "pigweed" and "fat hen." Other species are closely related to wild spinach. An example is the C. album which has existed for a very long time; however, it is difficult to determine its origination.

Wild spinach can be found worldwide but dominates the Northern Hemisphere. It is cultivated widely in Northern India as part of their delicacies.

When to Gather Wild Spinach

Around springtime, usually between April and May, several cultivated plants get seeded and are ready to get transplanted into the garden. Lamb quarters begin to germinate during this season in most places of North America. Because of the high rate at which they mature, they could compete with domesticated vegetables for nutrients from the soil and sunlight. Therefore, if not well monitored, lamb quarters could kill your veggies. You can harvest wild spinach between spring and midsummer because the leaves and stems are of their best quality.

Identifying Wild Spinach

The Leaves

The irregularly lobed leaves are easily distinguished from others by their arrangement, similar to a goose webbed foot; this is why some call it "goosefoot." Leaves grow in different patterns on a single stem and may have a whitish powder-like coating. Smaller leaves may have smoother edges, unlike larger leaves with toothed edges.

As shown in the picture above, the stem of a lamb quarter has little hairs and reddish stripes with streaks of green.

The Flowers

The flowers are small, with about five petals and stamens. The developing flowering stem, floret, is an excellent alternative to broccoli.

Growth Habit

Wild spinaches commonly grow to about three to five feet tall; some reach a length of over six feet. These plants are available throughout the year for harvest, unlike other plants that require a specific time or period of harvest. Plucking the tip of a large plant will trigger your wild spinach or lambs quarters to grow side shoots which would repopulate the area of land.

Harvesting and Storing

Unlike other delicate herbs like chickweed, lambs quarters are rugged herbs that survive any condition or abuse. Whenever you intend to harvest, pick out the young spinach yet to go to seed. You can cut off the greens from the plant using scissors and then place them in a paper bag. It is better to use a paper bag or plastic container if you are foraging wild spinach in the morning because the dew can tear up a paper bag.

After harvesting, the next step is to clean and revive them, especially after long hours, by dipping them in cool water. Fill your kitchen sink with water and spread the clusters of green into the water. Afterward, swish them gently for a few minutes so they can be refreshed and sturdy. Finally, place them in a towel and gently pat dry, then transfer them to a plastic bag or paper bag and refrigerate them till needed.

Plantain

This banana-like weed is a tropical plant (do not confuse it with tropical fruit) with completely edible and healthy leaves and seeds. When you are thinking of one of the perfect herbal cures for stings, mild skin injuries, and bug bites, this herb is one of them.

Where to Find Plantain

Plantains, scientifically known as Plantago, are commonly found in sunny areas with well-distributed fertile soil, like parks, lawns, and gardens.

Identifying Plantain

An easy way to identify plantains is to look out for the arrangement of the leaves. The leaves are usually arranged in a low circular formation called a low rosette. These leaves have a smooth edge and stretchy, prominent, and parallel veins. These veins are conspicuous, especially after detaching the leaves from the stem. You will find them poking out of the stalk-like little white threads.

Different species of plantains have unique features that make them easy to distinguish from one another. Plantago major, also known as common plantain, possess leaves that are oval in shape and wide. The leaves of P. rugelii, also known as Rugel's plantain, are also oval but have purplish or reddish coloration on the stalks. P. lanceolata, English or narrow-leaved plantain, has significantly narrow leaves (about an inch wide or less) and they grow to about a foot long or less.

The three plantain species possess flowers and seed heads that arise from the center of the leaf circular arrangement on the stalk. The seed heads of P.

lanceolata measure about one to two inches long with little white flowers. P. major and P. rugelii have seed heads that cover their stalks and spring out with green seeds that become brown or even black.

Harvesting and Drying

The good thing about plantain is that you can harvest them for as long as you wish, from spring through autumn. Do not hesitate to gather this widely spread herb, including the seeds. It is best to harvest the seeds after they become black or brown. Do not worry about the chaff that comes from the harvested seeds. Imagine them to be an added amount of fiber which they are.

Preserve your harvested plantain leaves by drying them with a dehydrator, making them ready for storage

Dock

Dock is a plant that grows anywhere and everywhere, especially in somewhat abandoned habitats or areas such as abandoned lots, gravel piles, etc.

This weed thrives well in the most unpleasant areas, like dumpsters, which prevents beginner foragers from trying to harvest and use the plant. The good news is they also develop well in decent environments. The plants are rugged and populous and grow throughout the year.

Identifying Dock

There are several species of completely edible docks around the world; a few examples are curly dock (Rumex crispus), field dock (R. pseudonatronatus), western dock (R. occidentalis), narrow leaf dock (R. stenophyllus), and patience dock (R. patientia). When it comes to the taste of the individual dock, people tend to prefer the patience dock over the others and even claim that it tastes the best. Regarding population, the curly dock is the most abundant, especially in the United States.

Like other docks, the perennial curly dock has a yellow taproot penetrating deeply into the ground. Its leaves are large, lance-shaped, elongated, and grow circularly on the ground. There is also a unique vein arrangement and prominent midrib that is lighter in color, running from top to bottom of the leaf. Another unique feature of this plant is that when you use your hands to break the leaves, you will have a slimy feeling on that hand.

Docks are populous in construction sites and bare sites. Their population tends to be low in areas with such human activities. Foraging for a dock is very easy, and because they appear in different forms year-round, understanding their peculiarities will help you quickly identify them.

During spring, dock leaves will start forming a circular arrangement, rosette. This usually begins from a central point and makes up the plant parts you can harvest. During late spring, the dock will begin to send up a beautiful flower stalk which will still permit the growth of leaves that are smaller and narrower than others. By this stage, the leaves beneath the stalks must be over a foot long.

Around the peak of summer, the flower stalk will become a seed head with a coffee-brown color. Unfortunately, the plant will end up dying once the numerous seeds which attain a pyramidal shape become fully ripe.

Finally, during the fall, the seemingly hopeless dead and dried stems will begin to spring up a new generation of fresh and tasty dock leaves. With that, you are sure of an early supply of forage for a long time before winter buries its beauty under the snow.

Harvesting Dock

The Leaves

Throughout its growing season, the dock leaves take on different appearances in shape, size, and texture but remain healthy to consume. The tender leaves are the best to harvest, and you can identify them by the crimp marks on the surface, which run from top to bottom. Dock leaves are quite tasty, and some people prefer to consume them raw, but others prefer to have them thoroughly cooked before consumption.

Even though most resources will tell foragers to target only the young leaf dock, it is advisable to use the older leaves. The major disadvantage of the older leaves is the bitter taste, making them terrible in a salad. The solution is to cook them smaller ones thoroughly to eliminate any bitterness. If you need to harvest the stem, remove the leaf tissue from the middle vein because it is often difficult to chew.

During the peak of its growing season, you can harvest as many dock leaves as you wish. They are the most abundant wild edibles after pokeweed.

The Flower Stalk

Remember the flower stalk mentioned earlier? They are also great for food as long as they are tender and not blooming. To prepare, you can chop it alongside the other parts of the plant for your stirfry recipe, or you can remove the leaves and peel off the tough outer layer of the stalk.

The Seeds

As regards dock seeds, they are dependent on individual preferences. Some prefer the seeds and even their taste to the leaves, while others find the taste of the seeds disgusting. The seeds can be eaten raw, dried, or roasted, depending on your preference.

Use the opportunity of foraging for docks to explore your taste. Find out if you will appreciate the taste of dock seeds or find them utterly disgusting. To harvest the seeds, run your hand through a seed head that has been dried properly and turned into a shade of brown. Immediately, the tiny buck weed-like seeds will fall into your hand.

Garlic Mustard

Where to Find it

This biennial plant is widespread in European and Asian regions, making them Eurasian wild edible. They can be found in the Midwestern United States, Alaska, Quebec, Alaska, Ontario, and British Columbia. They thrive well in areas with high human activities or disturbed places such as roadsides.

As a beginner forager, the best way to identify garlic mustard is during spring, when it begins to bloom. Depending on your location, you should expect this plant to bloom with flowers between the beginning to middle of May. When you are out foraging for some garlic mustard, look out for two to three-foot-tall herbaceous plants that appear precious and delicate. This plant should have little white flowers positioned on the leaves, as shown below.

Identifying Garlic Mustard

The Flowers

The attractive white flowers are small and appear in clusters on top of the plant. An individual flower with a diameter of one-half inches possesses no less than four petals.

The Leaves

The leaves appear heart-shaped, with lengths between 1.5 to 4 inches long, although there are variations in this appearance based on where they grow. They are also arranged in an alternating manner. The leaves at the bottom are also heart-shaped but have a blunt point with toothed edges. As you move up the plant stem, the leaves become more narrow, pointier, longer, and with scalloped edges.

The Seed Pods

By the middle to late May, you will find long skinny seed pods that are roughly one to three inches long appearing in the place where the flowers once occupied. Ripe seeds are somewhat elongated and dark in color.

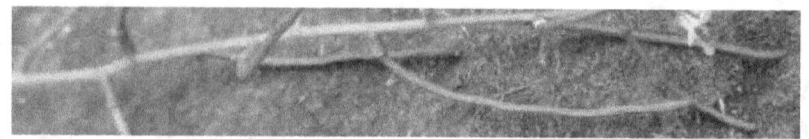

Harvesting Garlic Mustard

Stalks

It is believed that the best time to harvest the stalks is when they are still young and yet to flower. Some say young stalks taste better than mature ones. However, the description or taste preference varies from author to author. Some people taste like broccoli when eaten raw, while others believe they taste better when cooked. There is a possibility that the variation in taste might be due to taste buds, plant genetics, and maybe soil condition.

Leaves

The leaves are not bad themselves or bitter but have an intense and peppery flavor. The leaves only become astringent after the flowers have released their pods. Though, there is still a wide variation and description of the flavor from place to place. Some say it tastes like garlic, while some claim it tastes more like Mustard greens. However it is described, you are free to explore to arrive at your unique conclusion of how it tastes.

Miners Lettuce

What is Miner's Lettuce?

Miner's lettuce (Claytonia perfoliata) is a wild edible that is perfectly healthy to eat and delicious. A single taste of this plant will make you believe it is the best-tasting wild edible. Though it can be cooked alongside dishes, it is often eaten fresh in vegetable salads. This broadleaf plant grows annually in winter, or early spring, after heavy rainfall. It multiplies very fast and covers a wide expanse of land within a short time.

This plant got its name way back in the mid-1800s. During the California gold rush, many miners depended on this plant as a source of Vitamin C to prevent scurvy. It existed long before this gold rush period and was used by many people for food. It was commonly known as Indian lettuce or winter purslane, and it was a major food source for seedeating birds such as quail, mourning doves, etc. Even chickens find this plant incredibly tasty.

Where is Miner's Lettuce Native to?

Miner's lettuce is native to Canada and the Western United States. It is a natural inhabitant of Oregon, Washington, and California. However, it does not populate areas above 6600ft or low desert places. It is widely spread throughout British Columbia, Arizona, Central America, and Dakota. Utah, Wyoming, and Arizona states are not left out.

You may also find this plant growing in areas they are not native to, such as Cuba, New Zealand, Europe, Australia, and many other places. This edible weed has spread widely and is popular due to its pleasing taste.

Where Does Miner's Lettuce Grow?

Claytonia grows readily in cool and moist areas with lots of shades. In the west, you will find them inhabiting places like hillsides and riparian habitats or growing under trees in forests, chaparrals, and woodlands. You would also find them occupying farmlands, yards, and parks. Interestingly, they also grow alongside wild greens in winter, such as chickweed and nettles.

The ideal period to go foraging for some miner's lettuce is during winter and early spring, usually after a period of rainfall. This plant tends to shrivel up beneath hot weather, and they find it easy to repopulate an area of land by self-sowing.

Identifying Miner's Lettuce

After maturing, miner's lettuce is easy to recognize because they look like mini lilies with disclike leaves. The secondary leaves are large and round or may have a heart-shaped appearance surrounding the stem. They also have a cute little white flower in the middle. The primary leaves are smaller and are present before the larger, circular leaves form. When Claytonia starts to grow, it takes on a rosette-like appearance. This plant should not be confused with dollar weed which looks like it. The major difference is that the dollar weed has clusters of little flowers on different stems.

Young miner's lettuce seedlings:

A single Claytonia rosette or plant:

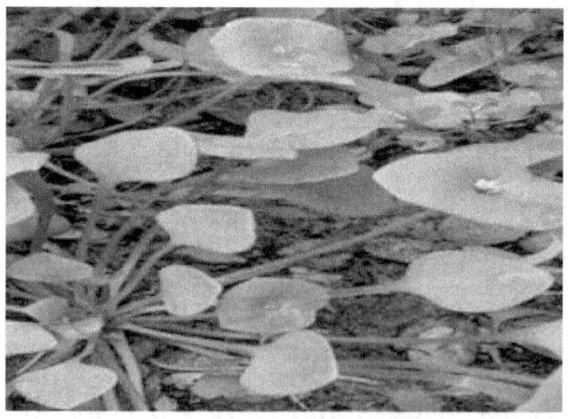

Miner's lettuce young primary leaves mixed with chickweed (the smallest leaves):

Miner's lettuce: secondary leaves and flowers:

What Does Miner's Lettuce Taste Like?

This edible herb has a very pleasant taste that is widely appreciated. Its sweet and earthy taste is closely associated with spinach. It has a crisp texture and is succulent, juicy, and tender. You can eat all the parts of the miner's lettuce, but the roots are not so delicious.

Is Miner's lettuce Good For You?

Since it was good for miners during the California gold rush, it is no doubt still nutritious and rich in vitamin C. According to research, there are also high quantities of vitamin A and trace levels of iron, calcium, protein, fiber, and omega-3 fatty acids. It also contains oxalic acid, which is also present in beans, almonds, potatoes, beets, and soy products. It is advisable to avoid eating miner's lettuce in excess because oxalate can be quite toxic when it binds with calcium, leading to the formation of kidney stones.

Harvesting Miner's Lettuce

To forage for miner's lettuce, selectively pick leaves and stems, leaving the developing rosette and roots to ensure a continuous supply. Be gentle and avoid over-harvesting. Forage in natural habitats, rinse before eating and harvest in the morning for maximum freshness. Store in the refrigerator with a sprinkle of water. Avoid harvesting in areas with human activity to prevent contamination.

Wild Violets

Where To Find Wild Violets

Foraging for wild violets can be easy or difficult, depending on the soil type. Even though they are rare, you can spot them easily in shady areas with moist soil. As long as the soil is dense with lots of moisture, they will thrive relatively well, even under full sunlight.

When Do Wild Violets Bloom?

Wild violets bloom in spring, especially in mild climates. Blooming is either by February or March; in some locations, they do not bloom until mid-May.

Identifying Wild Violets

There are different wild violet species with distinguishing characteristics. However, we will consider the viola sororia, a violet specie with purple, blue, or sometimes white blossom. This plant finds it easy to self-seed and repopulate, thereby finding its way into the wild.

The Flowers

Wild violet flowers have unique characteristics that make them stand out from others. Each flower always has petals that are no less or more than five and are shaped like a star. Two petals are directed upwards, another two points towards the sides, and the last petal points downwards.

When you look at the center of the flower closely, you will notice that it has streaks of a contrasting color. Each flower comes from a single leafless stalk emerging from the center of the parent plant. As regards color, blue or purple is usually associated with wild velvet flowers. However, they can come in yellow or white colors.

The Leaves

The leaves are heart-shaped with a very smooth texture. The leaves also curl slightly in the direction of the leaf stalk. Each wild violet leaf has its stem arising from the parent plant. When the violets are fully mature, these leaves attain a rich green color and become larger. However, the leaves become pretty small and light green when they grow under direct sunlight.

Violet Look-Alikes

The good thing about this wild plant is they don't have a direct lookalike. However, the heart-shaped leaves might be similar to some weeds. This is why it is advisable to be patient till they start to bloom before harvesting. Some people claim that violet leaves are a little similar to the poisonous Lesser Celandine and edible Marsh Marigold. Once again, it is best to have all violets bloom before harvesting them to avoid picking the wrong plant.

Harvesting Wild Violets

Your purpose of foraging for this wild edible will determine what part of the plant you wish to harvest. The flower and the leaves are both edible, but if harvesting for its healing property, then go for the leave.

Flowers are not just attractive but very delicious. However, they have a mild diuretic property. Harvesting the flowers should be done in the morning after the dew has dried, then using scissors, cut the flower at the flower's base (from the stem).

The leaves come with several indispensable health benefits. Firstly, they are very potent for lymphoid-related illnesses and maintainers of the lymphatic system. They can be used directly on the skin to treat skin inflammation, hives, rashes, and eczema. You can utilize the mucilage to promote digestion and treat cough and sore throat by ingesting the leaves. People appreciate the presence of this mucilage when eaten fresh, and some integrate it into their salads. Harvesting leaves is done similarly to how you'd harvest flowers.

Despite the numerous health benefits of the leaves, most people still prefer the flowers because it tastes better.

Drying and Storing Wild Violets

Drying the flowers of wild violets is done by air drying, i.e., laying them on a drying screen and then putting them in a ventilated area away from direct sunlight to dry up entirely (this will take roughly 4-7 days). Dried flowers can be stored in a tightly sealed container and kept in a cool dark spot.

Air drying is also the preferred method of drying the leaves of wild violets. To do this, simply gather a bunch of the leaves and use a rubber band to tie them, then hang them upside down to dry entirely. Have your leaves crunched up in your hands and store them in a container, setting aside in a cool dark area, such as your cupboard.

Cattail Shoots

Cattail, Typha latifolia, is a versatile plant found throughout the United States, particularly.

This plant thrives near bodies of water, and you can find it growing along waterways, in marshes, swamps, or in extremely wet soil. Once grown, it typically stands 5 to 8 feet tall. With its rigid, flat leaf stalks, it is simple to identify. An upright, rounded stem that can grow up to 6 or 7 feet (about 2 meters) tall can be found in the middle. Tiny male flowers are arranged in the upper cluster of the flower head, and tiny female flowers are arranged in the bottom cluster at the end of the stem. The male cluster appears bright golden when it is covered in pollen. The pollen is very simple to gather in big quantities.

The base of the stem can be consumed raw or cooked if picked at the appropriate time. Ensure the water is clean; avoid picking cattails in areas where there is a lot of human activity, horseback riding, etc., as the water may contain dangerous germs or even parasites.

The stem's base has a distinct leek-like appearance. Cut the lower stem with a knife, roughly 10 to 12 inches [20 to 25 centimeters] long, and put it in your foraging bag. Clean the stems completely once you get home; I typically use three water changes when cleaning the stems. To get to the delicate stalk, you might need to remove one or more layers of the very tender interior of the stem.

If you want to gather the starch-rich rhizomes, you'll need to get your hands soiled. I'm always interested in gathering the delicate, young white shoots that emerge from the root in the spring.

Early spring is typically the best time to gather cattail shoots, while May or June is the best time to collect pollen.

Foraging and Culinary Tips for Cattails

Roots

Cattail roots are found a few inches below the ground, and harvesting them can be messy. The roots are fibrous, spongy, and starchy. This starch can be extracted to make flour. You can chop the roots into small pieces, grind them in water, or scrape the starchy substance with a knife.

White shoots from cattail roots. Can be cooked, pickled, or eaten raw.

You can use the juice from the starch in primitive bread recipes, or the starch can be collected for future use. The young and tender white shoots that come out of the roots in spring are the delicacy. They can be cooked or pickled, sometimes cut into thick slices, and cooked like scallops with sauce at Melisse restaurant.

Shoots

The bottom end of cattail stalks can be eaten raw or cooked and has a leek-like appearance. It is often used in salads and has a flavor similar to cucumber with a nutty accent. The inner leaves can be easily accessed by pulling back the two main outer leaves, and the tender and edible parts are usually the first 4 to 10 inches, depending on various factors.

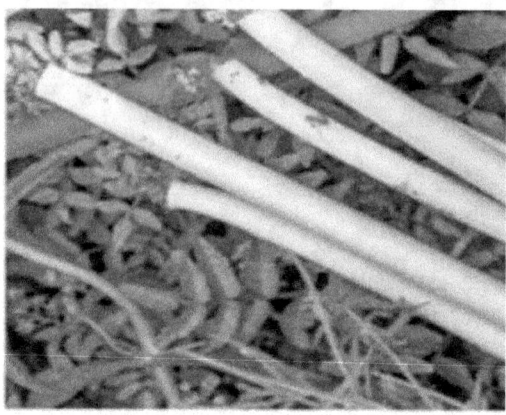

Tender cattail shoots. Can be cooked, pickled, or eaten raw.

Flowers

In Southern California, cattail pollen can be collected in May or June. The pollen can be used as yellow flour in bread and pastries. To remove the fluffy material mixed with the pollen, strain it using a regular kitchen strainer.

Male flower head loaded with pollen. Can be cooked when still green and pollen collected when yellow.

Green and immature female flower head. Boil for 15 to 20 minutes and eat like corn on the cob.

Dehydrate the pollen before storing it in a paper bag or jar to prevent molding. The bottom cluster of the cattail plant can be eaten like corn on the cob after boiling for 15 to 20 minutes, while the immature male flower can be boiled for 10 to 15 minutes and sautéed.

A Request from the Author:

Hey, I trust you're having a fascinating read. Please do share your feedback with me!

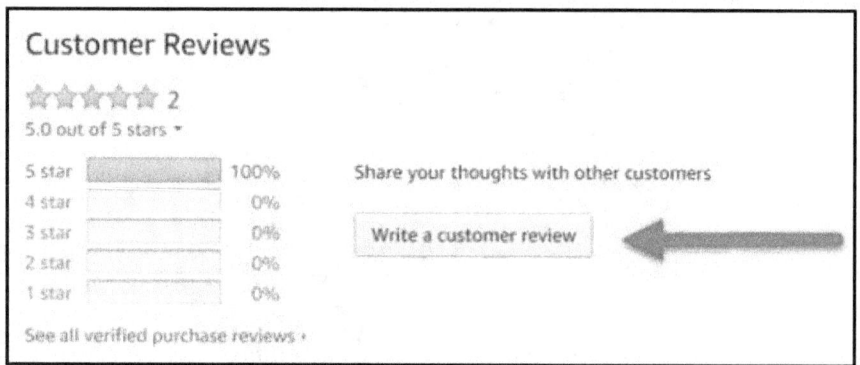

I'd be forever thankful if you could spend only 60 seconds writing a brief product review of this book on Amazon.

>> To post a brief review, click here.

Thanks so much.

Chapter 4

Foraging in Summer

Fireweed

Fireweed, also known as willow herb, is a colonist plant specie that effortlessly populates any area of land like roadsides, lawns, construction sites, etc. These plants can survive the strain and pressure of any environment or weather condition. The thin rose-colored flowers can transform an ugly landscape into one with stunning beauty.

Identifying Fireweed

One feature of the fireweed that makes it stand out easily is its impressive bright-colored flowers, usually pink or purple. These flowers have precisely four petals and look similar to some evening primrose species. Sometimes, after getting grazed by animals, they survive by making secondary flowers on a new branch to avoid extinction.

Another distinguishing feature of this plant is the ability of the flowers to start developing from the bottom of the stem before gently making their way to the top of the stem. The first bloom begins at the peak of summer, and the final boom occurs when the first bout of snow is about to start. This plant also blooms shortly before winter, so people embrace the fireweed with mixed feelings; it reminds them that winter is coming.

The fireweed fruits are thin but very long. After a while, this fruit will independently split open to release light, white seeds that soar into the wind. This plant grows on patches linked to one another by the roots. Its stem matures to a height of seven feet and is covered with leaves whose anterior part is dark green and whose posterior part has a silvery appearance. These willow-shaped leaves also have a light green central stem that runs through the length of the leaf. Unlike other plants, the lateral leaf vein does not reach the leaf's edge; but makes a loop on approaching the margin. With this feature, you can identify the fireweed, especially while they are still young.

When you go to logged or burned areas, you will most likely find fireweed as the dominant wild plant. They need a wet environment and excellent sunlight to thrive. You will also see them along clear cuts, roadsides, forest edges, and open fields.

Harvesting and Preparation

Fireweed offers unique importance or application at different growth stages. At their early stage of development, they can be eaten either raw or cooked. You should harvest the leaves while they are still pointing upwards and near the stem. You can harvest by snipping at the base with scissors or pinching off young leaves, which can be eaten like spinach. The older the plants get, the more unpalatable they are. The flower bud is also edible and can be used in salads.

The best period to harvest the leaves, especially for a rich-tasting tea, is when the plant flowers. To harvest, hold the stem a few centimeters below the flowers and pinch using your thumb and index finger. Push these fingers downwards to gather the fresh and rich green leaves.

Doing this will assist the plant in reseeding and encourage insects to enjoy the flower's nectar without hindrance. Next up, dry the leaves in paper bags or baskets and preserve them in a jar. They maintain their taste and quality all year round.

Eating Fireweed

Fireweed leaves are highly nutritious, containing flavonoids, vitamin C, and beta-carotene. They have a pleasant taste when eaten cooked or raw. They have a slippery liquid in them that makes them enjoyable to eat, especially while young. The older they get, the more fibrous their outer skin becomes. The plant's stalk can also be harvested and eaten as a treat by scrapping the mucilaginous pith, which is sometimes used as a thickener for dishes.

White Clover

White clover, Trifolium repens, is a perennial weed native to Europe, Central Asia, and some places in the middle east. This invasive plant is commonly found in lawns and quickly spreads over an area of land like a mat. They are easily identifiable by their white flowers and their trifoliate bright green leaves. The leaves are smooth, egg-shaped, with a whitish watermark figure shaped like a V.

White glover has a high nutritional value making them a good health booster. It has been used in the past as a blood cleanser and used to treat fevers. It is also applicable in the treatment of minor eye infections or discomfort. The leaves can relieve pain and inflammation from bruises, burns, and ulcers.

Harvesting White Clover

Pick out an area with minimal human activity to ensure safety from pesticides, herbicides, and possible animal waste. Also, take along your foraging materials, which include a bag, a small basket, an apron, and small scissors. To harvest, detach the flower heads from the plant stem using a pair of scissors.

After harvesting the clovers transfer them to a bowl or strainer and rinse properly to remove dirt and insects. Ensure to carry out this process gently because this plant is somewhat delicate and easily rips apart. Transfer the rinsed clover to a dish or flour sack towel and pat gently to remove excess moisture.

Preserving White Clover

You can preserve white glover effectively by dehydration. There are several ways to dehydrate white clover. You can place them in an electric dehydrator or on a baking rack to dry naturally using direct sunlight or a solar oven which has proven to be very effective.

The solar oven shown above is highly efficient and fast. To use, place a baking sheet or parchment paper over the baking rack and place it carefully in the solar oven. Pour your rinsed clover blossom on the paper, close the lid, open the reflectors, and wait for the final result.

After drying, store the clover blossoms in canned mason jars or airtight bags. You can be sure of having a constant supply of quality dried clover blossoms for a long time.

Elderberry

Elderberry, known as Sambucus, is a historic plant popular among older European traditions. They are very effective for the treatment of colds and flu. You can forage elderberries in wild spaces or cultivate them at the edge of your garden for easy harvesting.

Elderberries grow well during summer and become ripe after their flowers blossom in about three months. Elderberries in warmer climates tend to bloom earlier by June, unlike those in colder climates that start late in September.

Several species of elderberries could get you confused. However, each elderberry species differ based on environment and climatic conditions. An example of such specie native to California is the blue elderberries, botanically called Sambucus cerulea.

Even though elderberries are medicinal, you should watch out for the unripe ones, which include their leaves, berries, and stems, because they can be very toxic. Raw elderberries, in particular, have a bitter taste and are capable of causing stomach discomfort. However, you can improve their taste and effect by cooking them. In addition, ensure you avoid red berries because they are toxic to the body when eaten either ripe or unripe.

Finding Elderberries

You can find different species of elderberries all around Europe and North America. They grow effortlessly sideways, in backyards, and under shades. You can also see them growing close to wetlands like creeks and riverbanks.

Identifying Elderberry

This is a small tree that has either a single trunk or several trunks. Since they grow by the sucker, they often cramp themselves together, especially beneath a shade. The hollow stems have a pith within, which is visible when divided. The leaves of elderberries vary from one specie to another. For some, the leaves are a rich green color, having about five to nine leaflets with toothed edges. Others have black-colored and lacy leaves.

An elderberry tree has several clusters of berries, each having several berries. Each berry is small, about the width of a pencil. The berries of blue elderberries are not blue but have a white appearance due to the coatings of natural yeast. Some clusters are lucky enough to have berries of different colors, ranging from white and blue to black.

You might encounter an elderberry lookalike called Privet. This weed tree has berries that appear in clusters with colors like that of elderberry. The only way to differentiate this plant from the original is the cluster arrangement which is conical as compared to the flat arrangement of elderberry clusters. Also, you can identify elderberries by watching out for weed trees with constant visits from birds. If you find birds constantly attracted to a particular bush, you can be confident that you have found the elderberry bush.

Harvesting Elderberry

Harvesting elderberry is a fun activity. With a pruner, detach the berry clusters from the cluster stems. Do not forget that the stems and leaves of this bush are unhealthy for human consumption. Target berries that are shiny and have a plump appearance. Avoid unripe (green) and dry berries. Before cutting the cluster off the stem, give it a vigorous shake to remove bugs and dried berries.

Processing Elderberry

After gathering the berries, rinse them properly to remove dirt. You can do that by immersing the cluster in a bowl of water and swirling them around. After cleaning, the next task is to do something called garbling. It involves removing all other parts of this plant asides from the berries, which includes the stems, leaves, and debris. This step is not enjoyable for most people and can be stressful but unavoidable. You don't have to pick out the berries one after the other. Run your fingers through a cluster and get out as many berries as possible.

Drying

To dry the elderberries, spread them on a clean cookie sheet and cover them with a pop-up tent or picnic dishes to protect them from flies and insects. You can also use a dehydrator or dry in a low-temperature oven. The berries should dry thoroughly within a day.

Freezing

Freezing elderberries ensures they stay fresh for a long period. Spread the clean elderberries on a cookie sheet, ensuring they are in a single layer, and freeze. You also have the option of processing the berries and freezing the juice. Do this by cooking the berries gently on low heat and mash with a spoon to expel the juice.

The final processing involves transferring the mashed elderberries to cheesecloth and pressing to separate the juice from the chaff. Afterward, freeze it in a plastic bag or container. Eight cups of berries will give you about two cups of fresh juice.

Using Elderberry

Elderberry is known to have antiviral properties and boosts the immune system. It is excellent in treating viral infections such as upper respiratory infections, herpes, and the common cold. You can integrate the berries in pies, jam, and pastries. Eating the berries raw is not palatable, so cook them thoroughly before eating.

Goldenrod

Goldenrod, Solidago spp, is a wild edible plant with bright yellow flowers blooming in late summer and autumn. There are over seventy-five species of goldenrod in the United States.

The commonly used goldenrod species which are popular for their numerous medicinal benefits include the Canada goldenrod (Solidago canadensis), sweet goldenrod (S. odora), giant goldenrod (S. gigantea), and European goldenrod (S. virgaurea).

The benefits of goldenrod blooms are not limited to humans alone; honey bees can also depend on this plant for food. Solidago species are effective in treating common allergies, flu, colds, kidney stones, and cholesterol problems. You can infuse this plant salve to relieve pains and aches.

Identifying Goldenrod

Goldenrod is a tall perennial plant with stems that are about two to five feet tall. They also have bright yellow flowers arranged in clusters. You can find them in meadows, sunny and dry areas. They are native to North America and different parts of the world.

The Flowers

The flowers grow together as a cluster with the shape of a pyramid. Each flower are very small with a rough appearance.

The Leaves

The leaves are narrow and long, shaped like a lance, and arranged alternately along the stem. The leaves of some species may have serrated edges while others may have smooth edges.

Uses of Goldenrod

All parts of this medicinal wild edible are useful. However, the flowers are mostly used for medicinal purposes. Goldenrod can be used to treat kidney stones, allergies, fever, cold, high cholesterol levels in the blood, and many others.

Harvesting, Drying, and Storing Goldenrod

The best time to harvest goldenrod flowers is on a dry, sunny day. Rainy or dewy weather might make harvesting difficult for you. However, if it's not dangerous, you can work with the temperature presented at that moment. A pair of scissors would be needed to break the tough stems. Target the top one-third of the plant that contains the flowering tops. Ensure to avoid pulling out the whole plant from the soil; leave the roots in the soil, to ensure they grow the next year.

After harvesting, remove the flowering tops and separate them from individual stems. Spread them on a drying screen in a single layer and leave them out to dry thoroughly. You can use a dehydrator to go the faster route.

Store your thoroughly dried goldenrod in a mason jar or paper bag. Keep them in a cool, dry place, away from direct sunlight. Dried herbs have a shelf life of about nine months to a year if kept under favorable conditions. These herbs give signs when it starts losing their potency; the color starts to fade and gives off a musty smell. When you notice these signs, you should throw them out as compost.

Wild Chokecherry

You might probably think this plant might mean trouble since it has the word "choke" in it. It is also known as bitter berry, which doesn't do justice to how delicious it tastes. Interestingly, it was popular among Native Americans for jelly and homemade wine. When eaten raw, they have an acidic taste, but a good preparation will leave you wanting more.

Chokecherries, Prunus virginiana, are members of the stone fruit family. They are also closely related to plums and cherries. Chokeberries produce fruits arranged in clusters large enough to be plucked by mammals. For example, dexterous raccoons pluck these berries and separate this fruit from its harmful seeds before eating.

Finding Chokecherries

Finding chokecherry is relatively easy. They grow well along roadsides and require constant exposure to direct sunlight to thrive. They populate well-exposed areas of land. The red fruit or berry is very easy to spot even from a distance, and they attain a deep red color when fully ripe.

Bright red chokecherries are not pleasant to taste. You have to exercise patience to enjoy the sweet-tasting deep red chokecherries. When you see the unripe berries in meadows or edges of woodlands, mark their position accurately. Check back probably later to confirm if they are ripe. You cannot afford to miss your opportunity because ripe chokecherries are difficult to spot. This could be because many people seize the slightest opportunity to harvest some sweet chokeberries, making them rare.

In some places, chokeberry starts growing between mid-August to early September. Once again, avoid unripe chokeberries because they taste so terrible that you may be scared of even tasting the sweet ripe berries.

Identifying Chokecherry

Two major features of chokecherries make them stand out from others. First, they are in groups or bunches, and second, they possess a single large seed. A plant that looks similar to chokecherry is the common buckthorn. The fruits from buckthorn might form s cluster on the central branch, but this is not always so. Buckthorn is also very toxic with sharp thorns, making it very different from the thornless chokecherry.

Chokecherry Fruit

Chokecherry fruits are small, round and have different colors for different stages of development. The colors go from light green and yellow to bright red and finally dark red when fully ripe. Some of these cherries become nearly dark in color depending on the time animals like raccoons feed on them.

Chokecherry Seeds

The seeds inside a chokecherry are quite large. It takes up almost half of the fruit and is harmful to the human body when eaten. The seeds are separated from the fruit by boiling for a short while. Afterward, the loose fruits are transferred to a colander to have the seeds properly filtered. You should ensure that the seeds do not stay long in the jelly otherwise, the whole preparation will end up in the trash.

If you wish to cultivate some chokecherry seeds, pick out uncooked seeds and set them aside. Note that chokecherry seeds need to spend time dormant in a cold environment before they can sprout. Simply store these seeds in a freezer for about three months before cultivating them. The raw fruit stored in a refrigerator can remain fresh throughout the winter season till you are ready to plant the seeds.

Chokecherry Leaves

Chokecherry leaves are long, about two to four inches long, and arranged alternately on the central stem. They have an oval appearance with a pointy tip and slightly toothed edges.

Chokecherry Bark

The bark of the chokecherry plant has small dimples that are slightly raised, similar to different cherry types found locally.

Are Chokecherries Toxic?

Chokecherries are safe to eat, but their seeds contain cyanide and can be toxic in large amounts. Native Americans pounded the boiled fruit and sun-dried it to denature the toxins in the seeds, allowing them to consume both the fruit and seeds safely. However, this method has not been scientifically proven. It is best to avoid the seeds and the leaves, bark, and stems of the chokecherry plant, as they can be deadly if consumed in large amounts.

Wild Huckleberry

This berry, also known as whortleberry, bilberry, or hurtleberry, is described as a forager's treasure. Late into summer, forgers venture into far mountains to search for the huckleberry. This plant can only be found in the wilderness, not in regular places like common berries.

They thrive excellently on acidic and infertile soils that are above sea level, making it difficult to cultivate them in your backyard or garden. If you manage to have them pop some cherries in your garden, you should expect a taste of zero quality compared to huckleberries of the wild.

The rarity of huckleberry makes it valuable and fun to forage. It is like a reward for many foragers. On your next foraging adventure, look out for some rare huckleberries that can make your day.

Identifying Huckleberry

Huckleberries are similar in appearance to cranberries and blueberries, and its shrub can grow to a height of two to three feet beneath direct sunlight and up to ten feet beneath shades. Features that make huckleberry differ from others include its little oblong leaves having a shiny appearance and measuring up to an inch to a little above an inch.

They grow white, pink, or red flowers in early spring arranged in clusters. Huckleberry fruit varies from specie to species; their colors range from red, blue, purple, and black color. They are also small, about half an inch, and contain up to ten tiny seeds.

Huckleberries can easily be confused with blueberries. However, their sizes are very small when compared to blueberries. They also have a tart-like flavor that is extremely delicious.

Finding Wild Huckleberry

Huckleberries belong to two genera, Vaccinium and Gaylussacia, and different species can be found in unique habitats across North America. Whortleberry is found in Alberta, British Columbia, and other western states at high elevations, while Red Huckleberry thrives in forests, lowlands, and slopes along the West Coast.

California Huckleberry grows on dry slopes in foggy areas, while Black Huckleberry can be found in open areas in the eastern US. Dwarf Huckleberry is a low-growing shrub found in pine barrens and forests, and Blue Huckleberry occupies moist and dry woody areas, especially flatwoods with pines

Harvesting Huckleberries

Avoid plucking huckleberries while they are yet to mature because they cease to ripen after being separated from the parent plant. Ripe huckleberry fruits have a deep red color, full appearance, and very soft texture. Unripe huckleberries are tart-like, while ripe ones are sweet to taste.

To harvest huckleberries without posing damage to the bush, pick one at a time with your hands.

After harvesting, pour the berries into a large bowl and rinse them with cool tap water. Rinse thoroughly and drain using a colander, then dry them on a flat surface. Afterward, you can use them straightaway or refrigerate them for future use. Most people don't appreciate their berries sticking together after freezing. To prevent this, put them on a cookie sheet, ensuring they maintain a single layer, and set them in the freezer for roughly an hour before putting them in a jar.

Health Benefits of Wild Huckleberry

Huckleberries contain powerful polyphenols components with antioxidants that promote the overall health of humans. Experts in the Biomolecular and Clinical aspects of herbal medicine have discovered that anthocyanins from ripe huckleberry fruit are the most quickly absorbed. After an hour of ingestion, they quickly reach highly vascularized areas in the body, such as the brain, kidney, liver, and lungs.

The health benefits of eating huckleberry include healthy day and night vision, improved cell health, prevention of the risk of developing cancers or tumor cells, improved cardiovascular system, anti-inflammatory properties, and improved memory function.

Chapter 5

Foraging in Autumn

Burdock

Burdock is a popular medicinal herb that has been used for ages to treat various illnesses. It is native to Northern Asia and various parts of Europe. It is one of the core Chinese traditional medicine, famous for its effective treatment of respiratory illnesses and improving body function.

Finding Burdock Plants

These plants are famous for colonizing the edge of paths where animals and humans can easily pick and deposit their seeds. The seeds can reach other places by sticking to animal fur, clothes, and even shoes. They can easily stick to surfaces because of their spiky texture.

When to Harvest Burdock

Burdock is a biennial plant which makes the ideal time for harvesting the roots to be around fall, at the end of its initial growth, or during spring, when it would sprout. When it clocks two years of development, this plant utilizes the energy in its roots to produce tall flowers with very conspicuous spikes. It then starts to die by falling after producing sticky seed packets.

Burdock is usually harvested a few months after its growth due to its abundance, rapid growth pattern, and difficulty when harvesting the fully matured plant. By three months old, burdock already has several inches of beneficial taproot ready for harvest.

Identification

Basal leaves of greater burdock

Burdocks are tall plants with heights ranging from five to nine feet when fully matured. They also have basal leaves shaped like a triangle with a hairy base and arranged in a rosette-like pattern. These leaves also have a heart-shaped base and wavy edges. As the leaves go up the stalk, they get smaller and smaller. However, basal leaves can get three to four feet high. The flowers are tufts of punk to purple colors, which begin to seed during fall.

Differentiating Common and Greater Burdock

Flower heads of greater burdock   Flower heads of common burdock

There are two common burdock types; common and greater burdock. The greater burdock is tall with large leaves compared to the common burdock, with a small appearance. However, this is not a reliable way to differentiate between these two types because several factors, which include climate, environment, and soil type, affect the growth pattern of the burdock.

Common burdock has hollow leaves on its lower stem with a little groove in the center, while the greater burdock has a deep groove like celery. The flower stalk of the common burdock differs from the greater burdock by the extent of branching: the former branches very little while the latter branches extensively.

The flowerhead of the common burdock has an oval-shaped appearance and is generally stalkless, with a half to one-inch width. Greater burdocks have a larger spherical flowerhead, with a 1 to 1½ inches width, and grow on significantly long stalks.

Similar Species

There is a third burdock specie called the woolly burdock, Actium tomentosum.

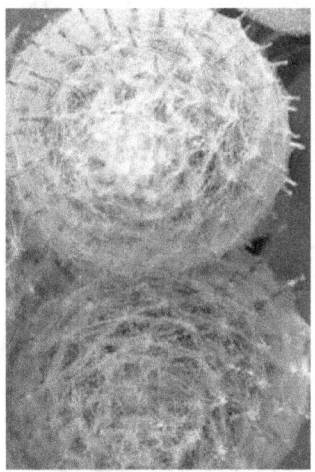

The flowerhead, leaf stems, and undersides have lots of web-like hairs. They occupy a few places in Canada, such as Quebec and Alberta. They also occupy areas in the United States like Maryland, North Dakota, Carolina, Illinois, and Oregon.

There is a fourth specie called the woodland burdock, Artium Vulgare, which is quite similar to the common burdock.

Look-Alikes

Burdock resembles rhubarb because they share properties like large triangle-shaped leaves.

However, the rhubarb leaf stem has a much reddish appearance compared to the burdock stem, with just streaks of maroon color. Also, the rhubarb leaf stem has a smooth and glossy appearance, while the hollow burdock leaf stem has a groovy appearance.

How to Harvest and Preserve Burdock

Burdock is a versatile plant with edible and medicinal properties. Almost all parts of the plant are edible, including the stems, flower stalk, and roots. The leaves are bitter but tolerable, while the stem leaves are slightly bitter and more tolerable. The flower stalk has a sweet flavor and texture similar to the stem leaves.

The roots, the best part of the plant to eat, can be harvested in the first year for a stalkless plant during the fall or in the second year before the plant produces a flower stalk. Burdock is challenging to eradicate due to its deep taproots, but digging a hole around the roots with a shovel makes it easier to harvest.

First, to preserve your harvested burdock roots, wash them, cut them into compact lengths, and dry them on screens in a dark but well-ventilated location.

Afterward, store them in plastic bags or jars to use much later.

Rose Hips

Rose hips are the oblong or round-shaped fruits of the popular rose plant. Rose flowers that are not picked before the flower fades will become a berry-like hip. Their colors range from red to orange. They are very similar to the size of a grape, with a firm texture. Inside the hips are several rose seeds and fizzy hairs.

Rose species, including the shrub rose, produce edible and medicinally beneficial hips. Shrub roses, such as Rosa rugosa, can be found in the wild, particularly in coastal dune climates, New England coasts, and some parts of the Pacific Northwest. These species offer a great foraging experience and are known to produce the best-tasting hips.

Where to Find Rose Hips

Rose hips are not difficult to locate because they can grow well regardless of soil conditions. Beach roses, as the name implies, grow on beaches or coastlines. Other species occupy parks, woods, roadsides, and private lands. They are rugged plants that withstand even the toughest climatic conditions like wind, cold, and heat. It is tough to eliminate due to its invasive or weedlike nature,

When to Find Rose Hips

The fruits of the rose plant are what we recognize as rose hips, and they appear after the blooms have detached from the parent plants. Rose hips start to mature from the start of fall till winter.

Identifying Rose Hips

Rose hips, the fruits of the rose plant, replace the fallen flowers once the temperature drops. Their color ranges from red to orange and is round-shaped or oblong, with little strands of hair emerging from beneath the fruit. There are various shapes and sizes of rosehips, such as the dog rose, which has a very oblong shape. Those that are larger with a more rounded appearance are the rugosa roses.

Harvesting Rose Hips

It is advisable to start harvesting rose hips in the fall. Rose hips become increasingly sweeter when they spend more time on the plant and get exposed to freezing temperatures. They might become wrinkled, but that should not be a problem. Also, target rose hips that are red to orange vine color because they are easy to remove from the stem.

After harvesting, you can use them immediately or store them in a freezer to increase their shelf life. You can also dry them by cutting the large rose hips open and then extracting the seeds and hairs before putting them in a dehydrator or flat screen to dry.

Edible Uses of Rose Hips

Rose hips are recognized as one of the plants with the highest quantity of vitamin C, especially when taken fresh. They taste like crab apples which have a sweet tart-like flavor. Within the rosehips are thready hairs that can irritate the stomach and throat when eaten. When processing rose hips, ensure it is thoroughly filtered using several layers of cheesecloth before serving. However, if you intend to eat rose hips whole, cut them open and remove the seeds and irritating hairs before using them. Rosehip is also used as a flavor in cocktails, whiskies, and other drinks.

Jerusalem Artichoke

Jerusalem artichokes are not from Jerusalem, and neither are they artichokes. Interesting right? However, they are members of the Asteraceae family and resemble a particular wild sunflower specie called Helianthus tuberosus. Also, it possesses tubers that look like ginger and has the sweet taste of a potato. The original name of this plant is Girasole, which means "turning in the direction of the sun." Because of this, some people prefer to call it sunchokes.

The other names of Jerusalem artichokes you might probably come across in the grocery store include earth apple, sun root, and sometimes Jerusalem fartichoke.

Identification

Jerusalem artichokes are typically large sunflowers with a height of up to twelve feet. Its leaves have an ovate appearance and can grow to a height of eight inches and a width of three inches. The leaves also have a rough texture which is the same as the artichoke stem.

The flowers bloom beautifully with a bright yellow color between August and September. They are about one to four inches wide and have fifteen to twenty petals. Finally, the roots consist of edible tubers with a reddish-to-whitish appearance.

Habitat

Sunchokes thrive well on neutral to slightly alkaline fertile soil consisting of organic matter to aid the rapid growth of tuber.

Harvesting

The ideal period to harvest Jerusalem artichokes is between mid to late fall. To harvest the roots, use a shovel to dig the soil and loosen the tubers with your hands. It is advisable to harvest sunchokes during winter because the freezing temperatures transform the insulin present in the sunchoke to fructose, which makes it so delicious.

Harvesting them too early will only give you artichokes that are difficult to digest, causing stomach upset. Another thing to note is that when digging, try to avoid bruising the tubers unless you intend to use them immediately. Bruised tubers get spoilt, making them unhealthy to eat and cultivate. It is best to leave sunchokes in the ground till you are ready to use them.

Cleaning

To clean sunchokes, simply rinse off the dirt under running water and aid the cleaning by scrubbing gently with a vegetable brush. To make the cleaning process easier, you can cut them into sections to thoroughly get rid of dirt in the curves and folds of the tubers. After cutting the tuber, its flesh will start darkening. So ensure you cook or eat immediately.

Storing

If you can't leave them in the ground or use all the harvested tubers immediately, you can store them in your freezer for about a week or two. Before transferring them to the freezer, ensure they are staked in a paper bag. They can stay fresh for up to a month under temperatures above freezing.

Hazelnut

Hazelnut is a wild edible that is loved by many. They make an excellent snack rich in fat, proteins, and flavors. Two popular hazelnut species are peculiar to North America; the American Hazel and Beaked Hazel. They are easy to come across, so foraging for hazelnut is like shopping at the grocery store, except that one is more adventurous.

Where and When to Find Hazelnuts

Hazelnuts are easy to locate, thriving well in hedgerows, woodlands, and scrubs. They begin to mature or ripen between late summer to early autumn.

How to Identify Hazel

This is a deciduous plant with a characteristic grey trunk and smooth texture. Its leaves are oval to round with serrated edges. The flowers are grouped into male and female. To identify the male flowers, look for low-hanging green catkins that open up during winter to produce pale yellow flowers. The female flowers are very tiny as compared to the male. It also has a collection of delicate tendrils arising from the top, which are bright red.

The hazelnut themselves are green in color when unripe with a papery covering. When ripe, their sheath transforms to brown and falls from the tree.

How to Harvest Wild Hazelnuts

When hazelnut begins to ripen, they turn into a shade of brown, while their involucres remain green. It is best to pick the nuts at this stage because waiting till the involucres become brown will cause them to fall to the ground and get eaten or crushed by animals.

To harvest American hazelnuts from its bush, pull out the entire clusters or pick out the nut directly from the involucres. It is best to wait for the clusters to dry thoroughly for a few days before removing the nuts.

Preserving

After harvesting hazelnuts, you can dry them to increase their shelf life. When the clusters are dry, separate the nuts from the bracts, spread them on trays maintaining a single layer, and keep them in a dry place away from sunlight. They should be fully dried after two or four weeks. You can hasten the drying process by using a dehydrator.

You can then store them shelled or unshelled in a refrigerator for up to a year. At room temperature, they last for not more than a month.

Acorns

The fall foraging season is usually welcomed with the presence of acorns. It is also a good season for squirrels who scurry here and there to gather as much as they can. The dense nutrients, including proteins, fats, and starches in these nuts, keep the squirrels healthy and help them survive the winter scarcity. Acorns are not for squirrels alone; several generations have also depended on this nutritious nut for survival.

Identifying Acorns

Acorns are the fruits of oak trees. An acorn's exterior is divided into two parts; the hard outer shell, called the pericarp, and the inner cap, called the cupule. The acorn stands out from other nuts because it looks like a seed or fruit putting on a hat.

There are diverse kinds of oak trees that breed different species of acorns. Also, it is quite difficult to differentiate between the various acorn species or oak trees. Thankfully, foragers need not worry because all acorn types are edible and healthy. Some are very palatable, and some are mildly tolerable.

There are two major oak tree species; the white oaks and the black or red oaks. These two oak trees can easily be differentiated from each other by their lobes. The white oaks have round-shaped and smooth textured lobes, while the black oaks have pointer lobes.

Acorn Foraging Tips

White oak acorns are less bitter than those from black or red oaks because their seeds mature in one season. The best time to gather acorns is from late September to late October, but they can also be found in parks and green spaces. When harvesting, use a mesh container to prevent molding and avoid picking up discolored or perforated acorns, which are signs of pest infestation and rot.

Sorting And Drying

Start by putting your harvested acorns in a big water bowl to separate the good from the bad. Any acorn that stays afloat should be disposed of because it indicates damage. After sorting and rinsing, dry the acorn with the fruit still in the shell for a short while. You can dry it with a dehydrator or heat from the sun. Drying will cause the nut to shrink, making it easier to separate it from the shell.

Shelling and Grinding

After drying, you can use diverse methods to crack them open. One of those methods involves making use of a hammer and woodblocks. To crack the acorn, place the pointy end on the woodblock and hit it on the rounded side using the hammer. Another method involves using heavy blocks to crack open several acorns at once.

Leaching

Remember that acorns have some tannins, which makes them astringent. To make them pleasant to eat, you must get rid of the tannins through leaching. This is done by soaking the acorns in water for hours or a few weeks, depending on the bitterness, and changing the water frequently till all the tannins are gone.

Processing the Haul

Remember to separate the white acorns from the black or red ones when collecting them. White acorns are less astringent with high water content, so endeavor to use them immediately because they can get spoilt if left unused for long. The black and red oaks require leaching before they can be edible.

If you don't intend to use them immediately, spread the acorns on a flat surface like an old baking pan, a bedspread, or a solar dehydrator where they can get fully aerated. Later, you may sight some weevil larvae boring out of the nut. That shouldn't faze you because even perfect-looking nuts might host these pests.

Chicory Root

Chicory is a perennial plant of the dandelion family that is surprisingly unpopular. It is commonly found growing along roadsides in several locations and usually goes unnoticed. Only a few people recognize chicory as an edible and highly medicinal plant.

Where and When to Forage for Chicory

Avoid harvesting any plant that grows along roadsides because those plants might be contaminated with oil or herbicides. Chicory is an invasive plant species that grows in areas with high human or industrial activities.

This plant has a close relation to the cultivated endive and radicchio species. Chicory leaves are bitter, but their quality health benefit is what makes it encouraging to eat. You can also cook them to reduce the bitterness.

The blooming season for chicory is usually between July and October. It gives out flowers with bluish to purplish appearance growing along a long stalk. These flowers open themselves to receive the morning sun, and sometimes all the flowers will close up at noon.

Uses for Chicory

This plant has existed for ages and is used to treat diverse illnesses, boost immunity and relieve stress symptoms. The roots are the most popularly used part of the chicory plant, foraged in the fall.

Harvesting chicory roots can be difficult because they grow in hard-packed soil. To make things easier, search for areas containing loose soil, or dig around the roots to harvest. The roots are edible, full of fiber and insulin, and a great source of probiotics. It is a good no-caffeinated substitute for coffee when roasted.

How to Identify Chicory

Chicory is an attractive and colorful plant that is worth cultivating. Even though all parts are edible, the main interest of most foragers is the roots. However, it is essential to know the distinguishing features of this plant, especially the leaves, because they look similar to some popular herbs.

The Leaves

The leaves are difficult to identify because they share some similar characteristics with several spring greens, like wild lettuce and dandelions. Chicory leaves are large, hairy, loved, and spread out at the bottom of the plant. The lobes decrease as they approach the tip of the leaf. The stems are covered with hairs as they branch out. The leaves decrease in size as they approach the tip of the stem, and each stem possess many blue or purple flowers.

The Flowers

This is the easiest part to recognize. Its beautiful blue/purple flower makes it stand out effortlessly. The petals are shaped like straps with parallel edges. This feature is also present in the yellow petals of dandelions (Thomas Elpel (2013)- Botany in a Day).

The Roots

The chicory root has a blackish appearance and several branches in its taproot, making it easy to distinguish from other chicory look-alikes.

Harvesting and Processing Chicory

After pulling out the roots from the soil, remove the stems and leaves, leaving only an inch of leaf base over the top of the root. Also, leave an inch of root too to replant to have a new population of chicory for spring. Afterward, wash the roots and ensure to scrub gently. To make things easier, harvest them after heavy rain because the rain would have softened the soil around the roots, making it easier to harvest. Also, soak them in water for about an hour to ease the cleaning process.

After cleaning properly, chop them into the same pieces, dry them, and heat them in an oven or iron pan. The taste gets better as the roast gets darker. You can blend the roasted root to make a cup of healthy coffee.

Chapter 6

Foraging in Winter

Beargrass

Bear grass (Xerophyllum Tenax), is so called because its stems are a food source for bears, and Grizzly bears use its leaves for their den. This plant is called Deer Grass, Elk Grass, Indian Basket Grass, and Soap grass. However, it is not actual grass.

Identifying Bear Grass

Bear grass is a herbaceous perennial plant belonging to the family of corn lilies. It develops from its seeds and rhizomes, which produce a lot of wirelike, curvy, and rigid leaves. These leaves can reach a height of up to three feet, with little serrated edges. Due to its tough structure, it can hold a significant amount of moisture to survive periods of drought and winter.

Beargrass takes so many years to mature. When it does, a tough flower stalk emerges from the central basal leaves and can grow to five feet. From this stalk, cream-colored flower crowns of different shapes emerge.

Where to Find Bear Grass

You can easily find beargrass growing as a native in the Pacific Northwest, specifically in California, Washington, and the rocky mountains. They grow well on slopes in fast-draining yet moist soil. They need a constant supply of sunlight to develop properly.

Beargrass require periodic burns to allow a new generation of stronger beargrass specie to grow.

Allowing the spread of a light fire will increase growing space, more room for light penetration, and higher soil nutrients. In addition, the fire-resistant rhizomes waste no time sprouting strong beargrass that starts flowering rapidly. It is usually the first plant to grow back after a period of fire.

Historical Use and Edibility

Beargrass was of great value for the Native Americans, who used the tough plant for decoration, weaving baskets, and making cloth and ropes. The tough leaves are used to create waterproof weaves. After drying, the leaves become white, and the flower stalk becomes a soft woof and is usually used to start a fire. This is essential for survivalists out in the wild who need to make a quick fire.

The roots were also of great value as they were roasted for food. Nowadays, they are usually boiled before eating. The roots can be very bitter to taste, but proper boiling and roasting can help remove excess bitterness. The seed pods are also edible only when they are yet to open.

Harvesting

Beargrass should be harvested in late June or later after the hardening of the new leaves. Grab the leaves you want to harvest, give them a swift twist, or use scissors to cut off the offshoots. Harvesting one-third of the new leaves ensures the continuity of this plant.

Hairy Bittercress

The name hairy bittercress does not justify how wonderful this wild edible tastes. This wild mustard has more of a spicy than bitter taste, and yet it is less spicy when compared to some plants of the Brassicaceae family. There are tiny hairs not easily visible on the stems and leaves. However, they are a little noticeable on the young bittercress.

This wild edible develops in the fall and starts to seed and flower during spring. This is why people consider the plant to be a winter annual.

Identification

The Leaves

Hairy bittercress has compound leaves that emerge from a basal rosette when young, and the mature leaves are divided into little leaflets arranged on either side of the central leaf stalk. Leaves that emerge from the red or green-colored flower stalks are narrower and longer than those from the main leaf stalk.

The Flowers

The flowers are tiny, about 2mm in size, and they start budding with not less than four sepals growing on a smooth stalk in the plant's central rosette. The mature white flower is shaped like a cross, hence its former family name, Cruciferae.

When hairy bittercress first blooms, only a single flower emerges from the flower stalk. After the flowers fully mature, the four petals fall off, leaving the seed pods. These seed pods will grow alongside the flower stalk, which will sprout new flowers later arranged alternately. These flowers develop in the direction of the plant's base stalk.

The Seeds

The green seed pods, siliques, become brown when they dry out. When they are fully dried, they explode, releasing their seeds in the process.

The Habitat

Hairy bittercress is an invasive plant that grows well beneath cool, dry weather. It dies in response to rising temperatures during late summer or spring, just like chickweed. It is one of the few plants that remain vibrantly green during winter and fall. Because of its love for well-distributed and moist soil, it is found growing in gardens and yards. They also grow along streams or naturally damp areas where they can get a constant water supply. Finally, you should avoid foraging for this plant in industrial areas because it may be contaminated with pathogens or harmful chemicals.

Weed control

Being an invasive plant, it can be a pain in the neck for gardeners. The best way to have these plants under control is to prevent their spread. You can do this by uprooting the plants during winter before they can start seeding. Each hairy bittercress is capable of producing between 600 to 1,000 seeds. So waiting till their seed pods explode to disperse these numerous seeds will only put your garden in danger.

You should also remove the plants from the roots to prevent the risk of repopulation. You can also maximize the delicious taste by making a healthy salad.

Range

This plant covers the whole southern and eastern United States alongside the West Coast.

Harvesting

Harvesting is very easy because it involves pulling out the plant by its roots from moist, loose soil. You can also harvest by cutting the leaf stalks, ensuring you steer clear of tough seedpods and flower stalks. Because the delicate leaves tend to wither easily, you should use them immediately.

Eating

This plant is a good source of vitamin C, and it has a flavor similar to watercress. You can use it as a substitute for microgreens in your salad, sandwich, or garnish. You can also blend the roots with vinegar to be used as a sauce or dip.

Peppergrass

Peppergrass (Lepidium spp.), belongs to the Brassica family and has over two species that grow in different parts of the world. They keep evolving to adapt to their ever-changing habitat. The popular peppergrass specie that is widely spread in Europe is the garden cress.

Virginia pepperweed (*Lepidium virginicum)*   Prairie peppergrass (*Lepidium densiflorum*)

In the United States, there are two common species; prairie peppergrass (Lepidium densiflorum) and Virginia pepperweed (Lepidium virginicum). These two are native to several states in the US. The Field pepperwort (Lepidium campestre) is another common plant native to Europe.

Foragers appreciate the plant for its peppery flavor. In the past, it was even considered the "poor man's pepper" because it was used as an alternative for those who couldn't afford actual pepper.

Identifying Peppergrass

Peppergrass stands out with its circularly arranged leaves with toothed edges. It also possesses a central stalk that bears little flowers arranged in clusters. Each cluster later matures into flattened and oval-shaped seed pods.

Foraging

The best time to forage for peppergrass is during the start of spring to mid-winter when its first shoots appear. The younger leaves have an excellent taste, but this doesn't stop the older leaves from being good for soups and dishes.

They grow in fields, yards, forests, disturbed soils, and woodlands. Ensure you avoid harvesting in busy areas or roads to prevent the risk of picking up herbs that might have been contaminated with harmful chemicals.

After foraging, ensure you wash them properly before consumption.

Edible Parts and Other Uses

The seed pods and their young leaves are edible, sweet-tasting, and spicy. They are perfect for salads or garnishes. The seeds themselves can be dried thoroughly for long-term use. All you need to do is, leave the stalks to dry in a cool place away from direct sunlight. Afterward, remove the seedpods and keep them in an airtight mason jar or container. They are great for adding spice to your recipes.

They have been used for ages to treat intestinal worms and vitamin deficiencies and have anti-inflammatory properties. Native Americans also utilized this herb in the treatment of respiratory illnesses. However, be cautious when eating this plant because a few people have reported having allergies after consuming this plant. If you are allergic to mustard, you should steer clear of peppergrass.

Peppergrass is regarded as a hyperaccumulator. This means it can absorb soil contents, which include toxins and nutrients. If the plant grows on soil that toxic metals have contaminated, it will absorb the metals effortlessly.

Juniper Berries

Juniper "berries" are cones and are very versatile. They can be used to flavor drinks, savory dishes, and desserts and can also be used medicinally or to make a sourdough starter. Juniper trees are common in the Northern Hemisphere and thrive in areas with extreme temperature variations and long periods of dry weather. If you live in areas where they grow, you may have picked an interest in them. However, juniper berries can easily be found in the wild.

Identifying Juniper

The "berries" of juniper trees are practically fleshy cones, not entirely resembling real berries, and are frequently draped in a fine, white bloom. The berries can be used in making a wild yeast starter for homebrewing since the bloom is, in fact, wild yeast!

When harvesting juniper cones for consumption or medicinal use, always be certain of the species you are harvesting because some species from Europe and China are poisonous. Overeating juniper berries from any species can also make you sick, so moderation is key.

If you are harvesting cones for propagation or decorative purposes, you don't have to worry about picking a toxic specie. It's also important to note that some cedars and cypresses look similar to junipers but can be distinguished by their berries and lack of pine-like smell.

How to Identify a Ripe Berry

To identify ripe juniper berries, tug on them to see if they give easily or are soft when squeezed. Most berries have a blue shade color when ripe, others white and indigo. This is why the color of the berry is not a reliable indicator unless you know the species and what color the ripe fruits are. It can take up to three years for juniper berries to mature, and not all berries on a tree will ripen at once.

Harvesting in fall and winter is recommended, but ripe berries can be harvested year-round, depending on the species. Fully ripe fruits may fall off the tree or be eaten by animals, so collecting them in time is important. However, if making traditional gin, wait until the cone is fully formed and mature in size but still green.

How to Harvest

To safely forage for juniper berries, avoid areas near roads and plants that have been sprayed with chemicals. It's best to hand-pick the berries, wearing gloves and protective clothing to avoid being stabbed by the plant's needles. If you come across a juniper you can identify, you can carefully and safely pull off the fruit even if you're not fully prepared. Use a basket or pouch to keep your hands free while picking.

Preservation and Storage

To make the fruits last longer, you can dry them in a food dehydrator or oven at a low temperature, but note that this may affect their flavor. Once dried, store them in a resealable jar in a cool, dry spot. Alternatively, you can store fresh fruits in a container with airflow, such as a canning jar with holes in the lid. Fresh fruits can last up to a year if stored properly, while dried fruits can last for years in a sealed container. Avoid direct sunlight for both.

Crab Apples

Crab apples are found across most of the US and some parts of Canada but not in Hawaii, Idaho, Arizona, and North Dakota. They are more common in the Eastern and Central US and can also be found in Quebec, Ontario, Manitoba, and British Columbia in Canada.

Crab apples are often planted ornamentally, so they may be found outside their natural range.

They can be found in various locations, such as parks, boulevards, yards, fields, hedgerows, and abandoned homesteads. There are ten native species in the US, including the prairie crab apple, which is native to Minnesota and can be found in thickets, forest edges, and grassy openings.

Identification

There are 25 species of crab apple in North America, and identifying them can be tricky due to hybridization. Crab apples are usually small trees or large shrubs with scaly, non-striped bark and oval-shaped leaves that grow on either side of their branch.

Crab apple flowers bloom in spring and are showy with five petals, making them common in landscaping. The flowers come in a range of colors, from red to pink to white. The fruit ripens in fall and can be yellow, orange, or red, and are typically smaller than two inches, with each fruit containing several small seeds. The bottom of the fruit may have a five-pointed sepal, but it often falls off before maturity.

Lookalikes

If you come across a fruit that looks and tastes like crab apple and is safe to eat, it's likely fine to eat, even if it's wild plum or hawthorn. While these fruits may resemble crab apples, there are differences in their trunks, seeds, and thorns that can help you distinguish them. Ultimately, if it looks and tastes like a crab apple, it's probably safe to eat.

Harvesting and Preparation

If you want to make a tasty crab apple paste, wait until winter when freezing temperatures make the apples sweet and soft, or freeze them for a few days if you pick them in the fall. To avoid wasting time, taste them first.

Harvesting them by hand is easy, and they fruit prolifically. You can use both small and large crab apples if they taste good. Wash and freeze them, then run them through a food mill, and add sweeteners and spices for flavor.

Caution

Crab apple seeds have amygdalin, which can turn into cyanide in the gut, but so do many other foods like apples and almonds. It would take a lot of seeds to cause harm. Scientific studies show that domesticated foods with amygdalin are safe, but monitoring is still recommended. There's no research on wild species, but it's unlikely to be a problem unless large amounts of crab apple seeds are consumed. To avoid toxicity, spit out the seeds or use a sieve or mill to process them.

The End... Almost!

Hey! This book has come to its last chapter, and I trust you've had a good read thus far.

As a self-published author with a limited advertising budget, I depend on you, my readers, to post a quick review of my book on Amazon because readers hardly post reviews.

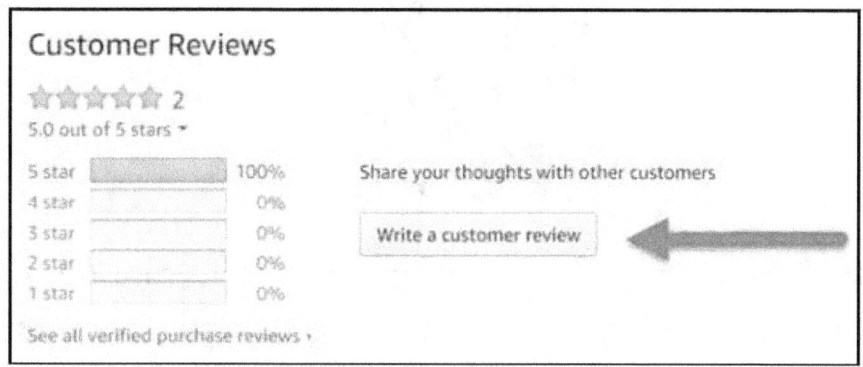

So, if you truly liked this book, would you kindly...

Submit a quick review on Amazon by clicking >> here.

Thanks so much.

Chapter 7

Edible Wild Plant Recipes

Violet Flower Syrup

Violet flower syrup is a delightful way to capture the essence of springtime in a bottle. This syrup is made by infusing fresh violet blossoms with a simple syrup solution, resulting in a sweet and floral flavor that can be used in a variety of desserts, drinks, and other culinary creations.

Ingredients:

- 1 cup violet flowers, lightly packed
- 1 cup water
- 1 cup white granulated sugar
- Fresh lemon juice

Instructions:

1. Pick your fresh violet flowers, removing any stems or leaves. Rinse the flowers gently in cold water, and allow them to dry completely.
2. Next, prepare the simple syrup solution by combining 2 cups of sugar and 2 cups of water in a large saucepan. Heat the mixture over medium heat, stirring occasionally, until the sugar has completely dissolved.
3. Once the sugar has dissolved, add the violet blossoms to the syrup and 1 tablespoon of lemon juice. Stir the mixture gently, ensuring all the flowers are fully submerged in the syrup.
4. Allow the mixture to simmer gently over low heat for about 15 minutes, stirring occasionally.

Remove the syrup from the heat, and allow it to cool completely.

5. Once the syrup has cooled, strain out the violet blossoms using a fine-mesh strainer or cheesecloth. Pour the syrup into a sterilized glass bottle or jar, and store it in the refrigerator for up to 2 weeks.

White Clover Iced Tea

White clover blossoms can be used to create a unique blend of refreshing iced tea, packed with nutrients that can rejuvenate your body.

Ingredients

- A cup of fresh white clover blossoms
- Honey (optional)
- Lemon wedge (optional)
- Water

Instructions:

1. Boil water in a jar for a few minutes, then add the blossoms and leave it undisturbed for about thirty minutes.
2. After the blossom contents have been extracted, serve with a clean fine mesh and store in the refrigerator.
3. You can now enjoy your iced tea cold, alongside maple syrup or honey to taste.

Chickweeds Pesto

Ingredients:

- ½ cup walnuts, cashews, or pine nuts
- 2-3 cloves garlic, minced
- 3 cups chickweed loosely packed
- 1 Tbsp lemon juice
- ½ cup extra virgin olive oil
- ½ tsp salt
- ¼ tsp freshly ground black pepper
- ¼ cup freshly grated Parmesan cheese

Equipment:

- Food Processor or Blender
- Refrigerator

Instructions:

1. Wash all fresh ingredients thoroughly.
2. Place all the ingredients into the food processor to ensure a smooth consistency.
3. If the paste is too thick, carefully add more olive oil.
4. After processing, you can eat it immediately or keep it refrigerated. Your pesto must be consumed within three to four days.

Acorn Soup

Acorns have been an important food source for humans for thousands of years. They are high in protein, healthy fats, and essential nutrients, making them a nutritious addition to any meal. One tasty way to enjoy the goodness of acorns is by making acorn soup. This simple recipe is easy to prepare and will satisfy your hunger while nourishing your body.

Ingredients:

- 2 to 3 cups acorn bits
- 1 carrot, peeled and chopped
- 2 celery stalks, chopped
- 1 medium onion, chopped
- 3 tablespoons butter
- 1 ounce dried porcini, soaked in 2 cups of hot water
- 2 bay leaves
- 1/3 cup brandy or bourbon
- 1-quart chicken, beef, mushroom, or vegetable stock
- Salt

Instructions:

1. To prepare this mushroom and acorn soup recipe, you will need to soak the dried mushrooms in hot water for an hour before cooking. Once the mushrooms are rehydrated, squeeze out excess moisture and chop them coarsely. Strain liquid and set it aside for later use.

2. Next, heat some butter in a soup pot over medium-high heat. Add chopped carrots, celery, and onions to the pot and sauté them until soft but not browned. This should take about 5 minutes. Then, add the chopped mushrooms and acorn bits and stir everything together. Cook for an additional.

3. Pour in some brandy and let it boil until it is almost evaporated. Then, add bay leaves, the reserved mushroom soaking water, and some stock. Bring the mixture to a simmer, taste for seasoning, and add salt if necessary. Cover the pot and let everything simmer gently for about an hour.

4. Once the soup is cooked, puree it in a blender or use an immersion blender until it is smooth. For a smoother texture, pass the soup through a fine-meshed sieve. If the soup is too thick, add more water or stock and simmer until it reaches the desired consistency.

5. To serve, drizzle some creme fraiche or sour cream over the soup and add chopped parsley and a few drops of your preferred oil, such as roasted squash seed oil. Add sliced grouse, partridge, pheasant, or chicken breast to the soup for a heartier meal. Enjoy this warm and comforting mushroom and acorn soup on a chilly day!

Chicory Mocha Coffee

Brew up a cup of delicious Chicory Mocha coffee naturally at home without spending a dime on expensive coffee houses with these few steps;

Ingredients:

- 2 tablespoons roasted chicory powder
- 1 cup water
- 1 cup of milk
- 1 tablespoon cocoa powder
- 1 teaspoon maple syrup (more or less to taste)

Instructions:

1. Combine the chicory powder and water in a saucepan and heat until boiling. Cover, lower the heat, and let it simmer for 10 minutes before straining the liquid.
2. Whisk together the cocoa powder, milk, and maple syrup in another saucepan over low heat. Once thoroughly combined, gently heat the mixture until it simmers, but be careful not to let it boil.

3. Next, add the strained chicory root coffee to the hot chocolate mixture and heat everything through.

4. Finally, pour the delicious mixture into a glass and enjoy it plain or with whipped cream. Savor the flavor and indulge in this perfect beverage's rich, creamy taste.

Acorn Pancakes

Taste a different pancake that is so exquisite from the conventional pancake you make at home with the following steps;

Ingredients:

- 1 cup flour
- 1 cup acorn meal
- 1 teaspoon salt
- 2 teaspoons baking powder
- 2 eggs
- ¼ cup of oil (vegetable or some other neutral-flavored type.)
- ½ cup honey
- 2 cups milk

Instructions:

1. To begin, heat the griddle to medium heat. Assemble all the dry ingredients into a large bowl.
2. Next, mix the oil, honey, eggs, and milk until the consistency is smooth. Combine the wet mixture with the dry ingredients in the large bowl. Adjust the batter by adding more milk if it's too thick or more flour if it's too thin.

3. Drop a small amount onto the griddle to test the batter and adjust the heat accordingly. Once you have the right temperature, use a ladle or spoon to pour dollar-sized pancakes onto the griddle. Cook until the bottom is browned and the top bubbles. This should not take more than three minutes. Flip and cook until the cakes are just firm to the touch.

4. Once the pancakes are done, transfer them to a warm plate. You can keep them in a warm oven covered with a towel until all the pancakes are finished.

Pickled Cattail Shoots

Enjoy a pickled cattail shoots right in the comfort of your home with these few recipes

Ingredients

- 8 medium-sized cattail shoots
- ¼ California bay leaf
- 2 small chili pods (optional)
- A teaspoon of sea salt

Pickling solutions:

- 3 cups of apple cider vinegar (5% acidity)
- 2 cups of sweet white wine or white elderberry wine (from Mexican elder)

Instructions:

1. To make pickled cattail shoots, begin by selecting the softest parts of the plant and cleaning them thoroughly. The outer layers may need to be removed, depending on the condition of the shoots. Next, sterilize the jars and keep them slightly warm by placing them in a shallow dish

of hot water. This will prevent the jars from cracking when the hot pickling solution is added.

2. Prepare the pickling solution, bringing it to a boil before slowly pouring it into the jars. Leave a half-inch of headspace in each jar, and use a clean spoon or knife to remove any air bubbles. As the cattail shoots tend to float, push them down gently before securing the lids.

3. Refrigerate the jars for at least two weeks before enjoying the pickled cattail shoots. Alternatively, the water bath method can be used to process the jars for 25 minutes in boiling water. Savor the unique flavor of this delicious and nutritious wild plant in your pickled cattail shoots.

Chokecherry Juice

Ingredients

- Wild Chokecherry

Instructions:

1. Begin by washing the berries after gathering them. Place the berries in a pot and add just enough water to cover them. Allow the berries to simmer for approximately 15 minutes, stirring occasionally. The flesh of the berries should easily separate from the seeds at this point.
2. Strain the contents of the pot through a fine mesh strainer and cheesecloth to remove the pits and collect the juice. The resulting juice will be cloudy and have a reddish-purple hue. Sweeten with sugar or honey as desired, or enjoy the juice as-is.
3. If you refrigerate the juice for a day or two, any sediment will settle to the bottom, and the juice will clear up. Add sugar or honey to taste, and savor chokecherries' delicious flavor and health benefits.

Garlic Mustard Pesto

Ingredients

- 2 cups of garlic mustard leaves, packed
- 1 cup of baby spinach leaves, packed
- ½ cup of walnuts or pine nuts
- ½ cup of grated Parmesan cheese
- ½ cup of extra-virgin olive oil
- 2 cloves of garlic, minced
- Salt and pepper to taste

Instructions:

1. Start by washing and drying the garlic mustard and baby spinach leaves.

2. In a food processor, pulse the garlic mustard, baby spinach, and walnuts (or pine nuts) until coarsely chopped.
3. Add the grated Parmesan cheese, minced garlic, salt, and pepper to the food processor, and pulse again until everything is combined.
4. While the food processor is running, slowly pour in the extra-virgin olive oil until the mixture becomes a smooth and creamy pesto.
5. Taste the pesto and adjust the seasoning as necessary.
6. Serve the Garlic Mustard Pesto over your favorite pasta, grilled meats, or vegetables, or use it as a dip or spread.

Roasted Jerusalem Artichoke

Ingredients:

- 1 pound Jerusalem artichokes (sunchokes), scrubbed and sliced into ¼ inch rounds
- 2 tablespoons olive oil
- 1 teaspoon garlic powder
- ½ teaspoon dried thyme
- Salt and pepper to taste

Instructions:

1. Preheat your oven to 350⁰C.
2. In a large bowl, toss the sliced Jerusalem artichokes with olive oil, garlic powder, dried thyme, salt, and pepper until evenly coated.
3. Spread the artichoke slices in a single layer on a baking sheet lined with parchment paper.
4. Roast the artichokes in the preheated oven for 25-30 minutes, or until they are tender and golden brown, flipping them over halfway through cooking.
5. Serve the roasted Jerusalem artichokes hot as a delicious and nutritious side dish.

6. Enjoy your flavorful and healthy roasted Jerusalem artichokes!

Burdock Flower Stalk Noodles

These burdock flower stalk noodles are delicious and packed with nutrients like fiber, iron, and potassium. This unique and wholesome twist on a classic dish will leave you feeling satisfied and nourished.

Ingredients:

- Four thick, six-inch sections of the burdock flower shoot, peeled and washed.

- Four cups of homemade vegetable stock
- Lemon juice
- Pinch of kosher salt

Instructions:

1. Begin by cleaning and preparing the burdock flowers and stalks, removing any dirt or debris. Slice the stalks into thin ribbons and chop the flowers finely. Sauté the burdock in a pan with a touch of oil until soft and fragrant.

2. Mix gluten-free flour, arrowroot powder, and a pinch of salt in a separate bowl. Create a well in the center of the mixture and add in the sautéed burdock along with a splash of water. Knead the dough until it becomes smooth and pliable.

3. Roll out the dough and cut it into your desired shape and size. Boil the noodles for a few minutes until they are tender, then serve with your favorite sauce or toppings.

Chokecherry Jam And Jelly

Ingredients:

- 4 cups of chokecherries, washed and stemmed
- 1 cup of water
- ¼ cup of lemon juice
- 1 ½ cups of granulated sugar
- 2 tablespoons of powdered pectin

Instructions:

1. Combine the chokecherries, water, and lemon juice in a large pot. Bring the mixture to a boil,

then reduce the heat to medium-low and simmer for 20 minutes, stirring occasionally.

2. Use a potato masher or immersion blender to mash the berries until they are broken down.

3. Pour the mixture through a fine mesh strainer or cheesecloth, discarding the solids.

4. Return the strained mixture to the pot and stir in the sugar and powdered pectin. Bring the mixture to a boil, stirring constantly.

5. Boil for 1-2 minutes until the mixture thickens and coats the back of a spoon.

6. Remove the pot from heat and ladle the jam into sterilized jars, leaving ¼ inch of headspace.

7. Store the jam in a cool, dry place for up to one year. Once opened, store in the refrigerator for up to three months.

Dandelion Shortbread Cookies

These dandelion shortbread cookies are a delicious and unique treat with a delicate floral flavor. Enjoy them with a cup of tea or as a sweet snack!

Ingredients:

- 1 cup unsalted butter, room temperature
- ½ cup powdered sugar
- 2 cups all-purpose flour
- ½ cup dandelion petals, washed and dried
- 1 teaspoon vanilla extract

Instructions:

1. Preheat your oven to 325°F (160°C).
2. Cream the butter and powdered sugar in a medium-sized bowl until light and fluffy.

3. Add the flour, dandelion petals, and vanilla extract to the butter mixture. Mix until well combined and a dough forms.
4. Roll the dough out on a floured surface to 1/4 inch thickness.
5. Cut the dough into your desired cookie shapes using a cookie cutter or knife.
6. Place the cookies on a parchment-lined baking sheet and bake for 15-20 minutes or until the edges are lightly golden.

Chokecherry Fruit Leather

Ingredients:

- 4 cups of very ripe chokecherries, washed and stemmed
- ½ cup water

Instructions:

1. In a large pot, combine the chokecherries and water. Bring the mixture to a boil, then reduce the

heat to low and simmer for 10-15 minutes or until the chokecherries are very soft and tender.

2. Remove the pot from the heat and use an immersion blender or potato masher to puree the chokecherries until smooth.

3. Pour the puree through a mesh food strainer to remove the seeds.

4. Enjoy your delicious and healthy chokecherry fruit leather as a snack or as a topping for oatmeal, yogurt, or ice cream!

Conclusion

The Pacific Northwest Foraging Field Guide is an excellent resource for beginners interested in exploring the wild edible plants of North America. This guidebook provides comprehensive information on finding, identifying, harvesting, and preparing a wide range of edible wild plants. It is an invaluable tool for those seeking to deepen their understanding and appreciation of the natural world.

With its detailed descriptions, vivid photographs, and practical tips, this guidebook will inspire you to embark on your own foraging adventures and discover the rich bounty of edible plants that the Pacific Northwest offers. Whether you are a seasoned forager or a curious beginner, this field guide is an essential addition to your library and a must-read for anyone interested in sustainable living and connecting with the natural world.